Southern Illinois University Press • Carbondale and Edwardsville

What Goes Around Comes Around

The Films of Jonathan Demme

Michael Bliss *&* Christina Banks

Library of Congress Cataloging-in-Publication Data

Bliss, Michael, 1947–
    What goes around comes around : the films of Jonathan Demme /
Michael Bliss and Christina Banks.
        p.   cm.
    Filmography : p.
    Includes bibliographical references and index.
    1. Demme, Jonathan, 1944-   —Criticism and interpretation.
I. Banks, Christina.   II. Title.
PN1998.3.D393B57   1996
791.43′0233′092—dc20
    ISBN 0-8093-1983-7   94-41204
    ISBN 0-8093-1984-5 pbk.   CIP

For Billy Gravening, in loving memory

Contents

Illustrations

Acknowledgments

The idea for this book originated with Christina Banks. After discussions with Banks, Michael Bliss wrote the book's rough draft with the exception of the chapter on *Who Am I This Time?* and the section on *Swing Shift*, which were written by Banks. The manuscript was then edited by Banks in consultation with Bliss and rewritten by Bliss. Bliss and Banks conducted the Demme interview; Craig McKay was interviewed by Michael Bliss.

Our thanks to Duane Perkins for the wonderful design job on the book; to Edward Saxon of Clinica Estetico for his cordial assistance; to Lucas Platt, formerly of Clinica Estetico, for his great help; to Ken Regan of Camera 5 for allowing us to use the photos from *Married to the Mob*, *The Silence of the Lambs*, and *Philadelphia*; to Neal Miller of Rubicon Film Productions for the still from *Who Am I This Time?*; to Terry Geedsen at the Museum of Modern Art Film Stills Library; to Michael Sragow and John L. Simons for useful criticism; and to Jonathan Demme for his graciousness and cooperation.

What Goes Around Comes Around

Introduction

Jonathan Demme is unique among American film directors. A graduate of what might be called the Roger Corman School of Filmmaking,[1] Demme quickly managed to outgrow his exploitation film background and establish himself as a director whose concern for humanistic issues and sensitivity to the newest, upbeat strains in contemporary music—along with a concurrent fascination with darker subjects—mark him as an impressive cinematic force. Known almost from the beginning of his career as a director whose politics were decidedly left of center, Demme made it clear even in his earliest films that his sympathies were with the poor and disadvantaged, that he was concerned with people of color and Third World countries[2] (a quality that emerges most pronouncedly in his documentaries *Haiti: Dreams of Democracy* [1987] and *Cousin Bobby* [1991]), and that he was interested in the manner in which strong female characters interact with various kinds of men in an attempt to create equitable, sustained relationships.

Born in 1944 in suburban Rockville Centre on Long Island and raised there and in Miami, Demme remembers developing a love of movies at an early age. "I don't know what it is, about the family structure or what, that makes a kid get so hooked on movies. When I was twelve or thirteen I'd go alone on the bus or train to see movies all over Long Island. I'd cut out ads—I had stacks of movie ads."[3] While attracted to the usual fare of Hollywood movies, Demme also liked the art films he went to with his parents.

Demme attended the University of Florida at Gainesville; his longtime intention of becoming a veterinarian defeated by his inability to do well in science classes, Demme quit school. As he remembers: "I started writing movie reviews for the college paper, and, as you know, when you start seeing movies free there's no going back. After I dropped out, I started reviewing for a local suburban weekly."[4] At this point, Demme's father, Robert Demme, who was the head publicist for Miami Beach's Fountainbleau hotel, introduced his son to producer Joseph E. Levine, whose houseboat was docked near the hotel. Levine, who was impressed with Demme's collection of advertising clips from, and reviews of, some of Levine's film releases (particularly *Zulu*), offered Demme a job as a press agent at Avco Embassy in New York. Next, Demme worked in London for a company producing commercials and as a rock correspondent for *Fusion*. He also made a short, called *Good Morning, Steve*. "A story so simple you barely noticed it: just a way of making a movie."[5] Eventually Demme was hired as publicist for *Von Richthofen and Brown*, a Roger Corman film being shot in Ireland.

Demme and his friend Joe Viola were then recruited by Corman to make B-movies. Demme remembers:

> After I did the publicity, Corman said, "Why don't you write a biker movie for my new company?" (He was just starting up New World Pictures.) Joe Viola and I worked on it and arranged to drop off the script at the London Hilton. As we were walking away, Roger called us back; he said, "Joe, you've directed commercials; why don't you direct the movie for me? And Jonathan, you've produced commercials; why don't you produce the movie?" That became *Angels Hard as They Come* [1971].[6]

Demme's first Corman films, formulaic and crude, were chiefly distinguished by the profuse amount of ambition and energy Demme brought to them. A significant amount of usable film had to be shot in a relatively short amount of time; Corman's directors learned to work fast and work economically.

One of the lessons that Demme says he learned from Corman was to always have something in the frame to which the eye could be attracted—some bit of information, some object or landscape.[7] It was during this period that Demme also realized how important it was to have a film that constantly kept moving, with no dead spots. Demme has remained true to this credo; the result is that most of his films play extremely well. At the studio preview of *The Silence of the Lambs*, the film seemed to move very quickly. And yet, weeks later, Demme and editor Craig McKay eliminated two of the film's scenes because they felt that they weren't sufficiently advancing the action.[8]

In interviews, Demme stresses the collaborative nature of filmmaking and declines to take full credit for his films. According to writer Roy Blount, Jr., Demme "doesn't like being focused on, because a movie involves many people working together."[9] Indeed, Demme is quick to bring up the contributions of those who work with him, evidence of a pronounced tendency away from egocentrism.

For the first Corman films that he directed, Demme wrote his own scripts. Demme says that he's not very good at writing,[10] although it may be that he's too hard on himself in this respect. The script for a prison-based film like *Caged Heat* manages to entertain us and still make significant points about the imbalance of power between men and women, the way that justice is skewed in favor of the rich, and the fact that American prisons seem to exemplify forms of political and sexual bias that occur elsewhere in the society.

Including a political aspect in his films for Corman was not as risky a quality for Demme as it might at first have seemed. Corman was perfectly willing to let his directors put "messages" into their films as long as those messages didn't conflict with the films' guiding principle: to keep the action going and the flesh showing. For Demme, though, his films' political dimension began to assume increasingly greater significance. Even in *Angels Hard as They Come*, one can see Demme incorporating into the film left-wing politics and a concern with nonwhite characters, thereby hinting at an orientation toward racial inclusiveness that will become one of the director's hallmark qualities. *The Hot Box* (1972, produced by Demme and cowritten with Joe Viola) inserts a burgeoning political awareness of Latin American repression and nationalist movements on the part of the film's American nurses (who have been kidnapped by revolutionaries) into what was, for the most part, an exploitation movie, while *Black Mama, White Mama* (1972), which was coscripted by Demme, demonstrates the director's inclusive sexual attitudes by remaking *The Defiant Ones* with women in the central roles. By the time of his first solo directorial venture for Corman, *Caged Heat* (1974), Demme was exploring the manner in which traditional paternalistic attitudes translate into social and economic oppression. In his second Corman feature, *Crazy Mama* (1975), Demme makes his analysis more probing: not just content to dramatize the effects of oppression, Demme searches for its causes. *Crazy Mama*, which depicts the misadventures of a family who've lost their farm, investigates and parodies American capitalism, which supports the kind of policies in evidence in *The Hot Box* and *Caged Heat*.

This critique on a political level, which reemerges in 1980's *Melvin and Howard*, seems for a time to be sidetracked in Demme's first independent film, *Citizens Band* (1977), a film centered on white, small-town America, which demonstrates another side of

Demme's personality: his concern with interpersonal relationships as microcosmic representations of national imbalances. Thus, the inability of *Citizens Band*'s characters to directly relate to one another may be read on a national level as one of the causes of the manipulative, unfeeling politics of the nation as a whole. As with *Crazy Mama*, Demme uses a national phenomenon (in this case the CB radio fad) to comment on the more extreme results of American individualism.

Demme's development in intellectual concerns is attended by a development in the director's control of the cinematic form. Indeed, right through to *Married to the Mob* (1988), we can trace in Demme's films a striking progress in technique, which may explain why *The Silence of the Lambs* (1991) in some ways seems like such an enigma, a technically accomplished production that is nonetheless atavistic from a moral and political point of view. At times, the film panders to the audience's desire for thrills and revenge (a consequence that to some extent results from the lurid subject matter), something that Demme has never done before and, judging by *Philadelphia* (1993), one hopes will never do again.

With the exception of *Silence of the Lambs*, which is concerned with a particularly American aberration, serial killers, and with regard to which Demme says that he was trying to deal with many dark aspects of our culture[11] (an area he had begun to explore in 1986's *Something Wild* and went on to examine in *Philadelphia*), Demme's films continue his stress on investigating the psychology underlying what it means to be an American, with attendant good-natured glances at the oddities of our society. Aside from the unsuccessful Hitchcock homage *Last Embrace* (1979), in which, despite a confused attempt to look at American Judaism, Demme's concern with culture seems to mysteriously disappear, Demme repeatedly tries to provide an answer to the question of what we can do to improve ourselves as individuals and as a nation.

Demme is just as genuine in his concern for the careers of emerging directors, many of whose interests mirror the kind of upbeat attitude that he brings to his own films. When Demme refused the offer to direct *Miami Blues* (he says he didn't want to follow one gangster film—*Married to the Mob*—with another),[12] he produced the film instead, turning over direction to George Armitage, with whom he had worked during his Corman period (Armitage and his family appear as bit players toward the end of *Caged Heat*). Demme also invested in *True Love*, a first film by Nancy Savoca, who worked as an assistant production auditor on *Something Wild* and *Married to the Mob*, and acted as executive producer of Savoca's *Household Saints*. In these actions, Demme shows that he believes in passing on his good fortune, thereby demonstrating the continuity between intention and practice toward which so many of his films' characters strive.

One of the indications of the pleasure that Demme takes in making movies is the fact that he has built up a large number of people, both actors and production staff, with whom he enjoys working and who go out of their way to work with him. While casting scripts, Demme invites character actors such as Charles Napier and Tracey Walter to pick out roles they'd like. Cinematographer Tak Fujimoto has been with Demme on most of his films since *Caged Heat*, and in the last few years production designer Kristi Zea, producers Kenneth Utt and Edward Saxon (both of whom have been drafted for small roles), and editor Craig McKay have worked with Demme on almost every film.

It is said of George Cukor that he was a "woman's director," in that Cukor had a facility for giving direction to actresses. Like Cukor, Demme elicits excellent performances from actresses (Melanie Griffith and Michelle Pfeiffer's best work has been for Demme). According to Demme, "Ever since my days working with Roger Corman, and perhaps before that, I've been a sucker for a women's picture. A film with a woman protagonist at the forefront. A woman in jeopardy. A woman on a mission. These are themes that have tremendous appeal to me as a moviegoer and also as a director."[13]

Demme may be said to be a female-oriented director in that his concerns seem to mirror those traditionally associated with women. Often, Demme is interested more in interpersonal relations than in action, in feelings rather than deeds, attitudes complemented by the director's focus on issues of sexual equality and justice.

Demme also distinguishes himself in his use of music. From his very first work, Demme incorporated contemporary music into his films to set moods and bolster his films' themes. However, since 1986, much of Demme's film music has been by progressive artists such as Laurie Anderson, Q Lazzarus, Chris Isaak, The Feelies, and David Byrne, with the result that the music never seems dated. Noteworthy as well is Demme's reliance on reggae, a heavily liberationist and upbeat music, as witnessed by the Ziggy Marley piece "Time Bums" in *Married to the Mob* and Jimmy Cliff's "You Don't Have To Cry" (a song that in Demme-like fashion links political exploitation and emotional depression) in *Something Wild*, a film that not only features reggae singer "Sister" Carol East in a dramatic role (she also appears in *Married*) but which ends its vocal music selections with "Sister" Carol's rendition of "Wild Thing."

Much of the effect of Demme's films derives from their feelings. Despite his occasionally dealing with violent material, Demme is nonetheless what could be immediately described as a gentle filmmaker. His affection for people shows through in the selection of the oddball characters with which he usually populates his films (the only evidence of this quality in *Silence of the Lambs* is the brief use of actor Paul Lazar as the somewhat comical Pilcher; no such characters appear in *Philadelphia*, although Joe Miller's repeated acts of self-promotion create a bit of humor). With the exception of the director-repudiated *Last Embrace*, the studio release version of *Swing Shift*, and *Silence of the Lambs*, the last of which was meant to be quite serious, you never see a Demme film without emerging from it feeling that it was created by someone who loves life and all of its funny occurrences, and who has a tender spot for all of the sweet things that can happen between people.

Demme's films often focus on an essentially moral young man. Despite his impracticality, *Melvin and Howard*'s Melvin Dummar is a genuinely nice person, as are *Citizens Band*'s Spider and *Something Wild*'s Charlie Driggs. These men not only care passionately about doing the right thing but also agonize about how to find the best way to get along with their women.

The female protagonists in Demme's films act as the films' thematic centers, providing impetus for events, admirably asserting themselves in the face of sometimes intimidating odds, as does Angela in *Married to the Mob*. Demme's women are strong individuals who want love and commitment and are willing to facilitate the changes in their men (in whom they recognize a potential for honesty and compassion) that are necessary to create a positive and life-affirming relationship. *Citizens Band*'s Pam and *Something Wild*'s Audrey may for a while indulge in activities that don't seem to work toward the achievement of this goal, but the truth is that what these women are doing is protecting themselves from disappointment via the way that they mask their identities through assumed, tough personae (indeed, the assumption of masks, and their divestiture as a necessary prerequisite to enlightenment, is one of Demme's main themes). At the same time as they act under assumed guises, these women make it clear that they are seeking satisfaction of their need for some form of rewarding human contact.

As one might expect, the tendency of Demme's film women to tap into a life-affirming spirit is attended by some of their films' most upbeat music, which strikingly contrasts with the music that is thematically linked with the men in these films. Thus, the music associated with *Married to the Mob*'s Tony and Mike is grim compared with most of the music associated with Angela. Even the themes that David Byrne wrote especially for the characters demonstrate this quality: Tony's theme is dark and ominous, appropriate since he connotes death; Angela's theme, in which an organ's light strains predominate, is airy and hopeful.

If not female-inspired, the vital beat of Demme's film music is at the very least so strongly associated with life over death that you can't help but feel good when you're exposed to it (the exceptions are the music for *Last Embrace*, *Silence of the Lambs*, and *Philadelphia*, which is appropriately grim). When you combine these good feelings with the ones that Demme creates through his stories, the result is a series of films affirming life and love, a rarity in contemporary American filmmaking. Demme reinvokes the loveliness of screwball comedy but without its manic aspect, combines this quality with Capra's political populism and faith in people's essential goodness and Kubrick and Scorsese's mastery of form (but without these latter directors' prominent morbid characters), and blends all of these qualities with a Third World mix of pop, reggae, and left-of-center politics that makes Demme our most vibrant and enjoyable filmmaker.

Demme's films attest to the belief that a successful romantic relationship is a microcosmic representation of humanistic democratic principles. The people in these relationships have different needs and, often, quite different backgrounds, but they manage to work out their difficulties and create a positive mode of interaction. Charlie and Audrey in *Something Wild* are a case in point. Charlie represents straight white male Western society; Audrey, at least at the film's beginning, evidences an affinity for the darker side of existence as well as more exotic cultures. Essentially, though, each character wants the same things: love and compassion. Often, Demme places the members of his couples at opposite ends of the legal spectrum, as he does with Harry and Ellie in *Last Embrace* (both of whom are nonetheless intimately involved in murder), and Mike and Angela in *Married to the Mob*. Regardless of his characters' backgrounds, though, what we see in Demme's films is a classic sexual and political dialectic at work, a wedding of two opposite realms that yields a satisfying synthesis. What Demme seems to be telling us is that entrenched cultural attitudes are rapidly dying, that the male principle requires the chastening effects of the life-affirmation traditionally associated with women, and that these two realms must reconcile in order for society to profitably continue. In *Philadelphia*, the paradigm reaches new sophistication. Although Demme is dealing with a unique kind of relationship for him, a homosexual one, he still stresses the need for love and commitment between Andy and Miguel, thereby demonstrating that his humanistic attitude is blind not only to differences in color or ethnic background (a carryover from *Black Mama, White Mama*) but is also equitably applied regardless of the character's sexual orientation.

Above all, what many of the characters in Demme's films strive for is a common language among people, a notion that in *Citizens Band* is expanded to include the need for self-knowledge as a prelude to an entire town's realization that it must communicate on both an individual and group level. In *Melvin and Howard*, Demme shows us the need for communication from the film's very beginning in the meeting between Melvin and a man claiming to be Howard Hughes; moreover, the film makes it clear that what is being investigated is the patchwork nature of American society itself. Indeed, no other filmmaker working today is as concerned with the idiosyncratic aspects of American culture as is Jonathan Demme. Demme takes pleasure in street singers, in a man who plays music with spoons, in a motorcyclist who takes his dog along with him for rides, in good-hearted, ambulance-chasing lawyers who aren't too ashamed to pursue a potential client who is on crutches—all of them people who express American individualism at its unselfconscious best.

Although Demme's interests seem to emerge naturally from the material he chooses, his primary cinematic goal is to enjoy the filmmaking process and produce a movie that will challenge and please the audience. Demme's open-mindedness and comprehensive appreciation of life may help explain his willingness to include dark aspects in his predominantly light vision.

One way of focusing on this dark quality in the director's work is to draw attention to a novel that Demme wanted to make into a film but for which an acceptable script was never completed: Don De-Lillo's *Libra*, which Demme planned to put into production after completing *Married to the Mob*. *Libra* is the story of Lee Harvey Oswald, with specific reference to Oswald's involvement in the assassination of John F. Kennedy. While one can see in the project the characteristic Demme concern with politics, it seems likely that it was the convoluted psychology of *Libra*'s Oswald that most fascinated the director; a comparable interest is apparent in productions such as *Something Wild*, *Married to the Mob*, and *Silence of the Lambs*, all of which feature psychopathic characters.

In *Libra*, DeLillo focuses on what he elsewhere referred to as "the dark center of the assassination,"[14] by which he seems to mean not just the mystery surrounding the conflicting explanations for the events in Dallas on November 22, 1963, but also the motivations of Oswald himself. DeLillo investigates and dramatizes the psychologies of men like Oswald, possible right-wing conspirator David Ferrie and—in an anticipation of the structure of *Silence of the Lambs*, which pits the supposedly reasonable government world against the shadow existence of Jame Gumb—fictional CIA agent Win Everett, who is involved more than a bit tangentially in the activities of the various men who converge on Dallas.

Describing Oswald in an interview, DeLillo might just as well be providing a capsule description of many of the fringe element characters in Demme's films, from *Caged Heat*'s Pandora to *Crazy Mama*'s Melba, from the crazed gunman in *Melvin and Howard* to *Something Wild*'s Ray, *Silence of the Lambs*'s Jame Gumb, and, to an extent, *Philadelphia*'s Andy Beckett.

> I think I have an idea of what it's like to be an outsider in this society. Oswald was clearly an outsider, although he fought against his exclusion. I had a very haunting sense of what kind of life he led and what kind of person he was. I experienced it when I saw the places where he lived in New Orleans and Dallas and in Fort Worth. I had a very clear sense of a man living on the margins of society.[15]

When DeLillo goes on to refer to Oswald's "life in small rooms," which he conceives of as "the antithesis of the life that America seems to promise its citizens: the life of consumer fulfillment,"[16] he inadvertently provides an accurate description of Demme's concern with people who seem to feel that they can be redeemed through conspicuous consumption (a trait most prevalent in the gross acquisitiveness of *Married to the Mob*'s gang members, but which is also true of Melvin Dummar), and of the sense of alienation that so many of the disappointed characters in Demme's films (Gumb most prominently) seem to evince.

Demme has always demonstrated an interest in the marginalized aspects of American culture, but he has never drawn a direct correlation between consumerism and violence. Nonetheless, DeLillo's hypothesis about the linkage between these two realms provides one way of understanding why the violent characters in films like *Something Wild* and *Married to the Mob* act the way that they do.

In a letter to his brother that is used as the headnote to *Libra*, Lee Oswald expressed the need for some form of belonging. "Happiness is not based on oneself, it does not consist of a small home, of taking and getting. Happiness is taking part in the struggle, where there is no borderline between one's personal world, and the world in general."[17] Yet Oswald, like Gumb (who initially worked through the system—in this case, the medical establishment—in trying to achieve his ends), ultimately resorted to premeditated violence in an attempt to get what he wanted. However, it is important to note that in Demme's work, violence doesn't usually inhere in the films' central characters. These individuals—Jacqueline in *Caged Heat*, Melvin Dummar, Audrey and Charlie, Angela, *Silence of the Lambs*'s Clarice—come in contact with violence but are not themselves violent people, although, like Charlie and Clarice, they may ultimately resort to violence in order to subdue it.

The notion of an essentially nonviolent individual defeating a violent counterpart brings up the theme of the doppelganger, a notion prevalent in Demme's work in doubles such as Jacqueline and Pandora, Mike and Tony, and Clarice and Lecter.[18] As we might expect, doubles in Demme's films sometimes occur not only as externally realized others but also as representatives of a certain character's alternate state of mind (for example, *Something Wild*'s Ray as Charlie's dark side). We can even see these opposing tendencies in a film as superficially placid as *Citizens Band*, in which the entire town of Unity is operating in a dualistic mode: people seem to be one thing in person but manifest different personalities when they are on the radio.

One can see a strong affinity between this type of characterization and the work of Alfred Hitchcock, for whom Demme has repeatedly expressed admiration. The tracking point-of-view shots in *Married to the Mob*, the god's eye and point-of-view shots in *Something Wild* and *Silence of the Lambs*, and Demme's appearance in his own films (as "extras," he and his wife play tourists in both *Married to the Mob* and *Silence of the Lambs*)—all of these examples are further evidence of the Hitchcock influence.

The dualistic conception of character represents more than Demme's use of conflict as a dramatic device; what we also see expressed here is the director's belief that opposing tendencies inform the nature of the universe. Even the characters themselves feel the need for a kind of balance, hence the emphasis in Demme's work on the ideas and feelings associated with the individual discovering him- or herself through the group. Alternatively, as in *Who Am I This Time?*, characters find their identities by putting on the mask of another, fictional identity, a notion that looks forward not only to Audrey's changes of identity in *Something Wild* but also Gumb's assumption of the female persona when he dances in his basement.[19]

Like Jame Gumb, many of the dangerous characters in Demme's films seem to be defined through their violence. There seems to be a vacuum at the center of these characters, and we're suspicious when they're not violent (as we are of Ray when he's pretending to be nice). At the same time, though, these lonely and alienated people exhibit paradoxical tendencies because, again as with Oswald, who preferred that the " 'veil between him and other people . . . remain intact,' "[20] they appear to enjoy being the way they are. Like Oswald and the most prominent outsider in Demme's work, Ray, many of Demme's outlaw characters don't seem to have any identity outside of brutality.

Over time, Demme has begun to question the limits of screen violence.

> I think it's important to show that violence is truly awful. The struggle I have, which I don't think is present in [*Silence of the Lambs*] but is in *Married to the Mob*, is that even with my aversion to violence, the cineaste in me can't, for example, resist having Dean Stockwell come tumbling out of his car using a two-gun style to decimate guys in a scene that I hope looks like it's out of some Raoul Walsh movie from the forties. I also understand that in a sheer pleasure movie like *Married to the Mob*, it's important to entertain the audience. There I'm trying to walk a tightrope between making it exciting and not making it fun. I think I failed there; I fell into fun. . . . I'm not pleased with that, although I still enjoy those scenes. I'm very schizo on the subject.[21]

Simultaneous with the tendency toward violence, though, are the forces in Demme's films that seem to be strongly based on the principles of comedy. According to Northrop Frye, at the beginnings of comic stories is an anticomic society that is rigid and opposed to the comic urge toward freedom, and which works against the achievement of an ending that results in what Frye labels an anastrophe, a turning up as opposed to a turning down—in other words, a movement toward hope instead of despair.[22] This anastrophe, which sometimes involves the celebration of a public rite (often a sacred marriage), is characterized by a social cohesion that Frye posits as the very hallmark of comedy. "The theme of the comic is the integration of society, which usually takes the form of incorporating a central character into it,"[23] an idea that is vital to Demme's notion of the necessity for community, regardless of whether community is achieved on a purely individual level (as in the final relationship between *Something Wild*'s Charlie and Audrey), or on the larger level of an entire town (the cohesion that occurs at the end of *Citizens Band*). Deliverance from a negative society into some form of communal bonding also fits this schema, which can be recognized in the form of the escape from prison in *Caged Heat*, the marriage that ends *Citizens Band*, the reorientation of the marriage of Kay and Jack in Demme's cut of *Swing Shift*, what looks like the imminent wedding of Mike and Angela in *Married to the Mob*, the celebratory ritualistic conferring of FBI status on *Silence of the Lambs*'s Clarice Starling in what essentially amounts to her sacred marriage to the bureau (an act that takes place after she has quelled the antisocial force represented by Gumb), and the triumph of *Philadelphia*'s Andy, who with regard to some of straight society is alienated and socially displaced.

Frye notes that the anticomic theme may also be expressed "by mood instead of (or along with) an element in the structure. Some of the comedies begin in a mood of deep melancholy,"[24] a situation that we can recognize in the social chaos in *Caged Heat*; Lulu's disruptive, almost irrational actions at the beginning of *Something Wild*; Angela's despair in *Married to the Mob*, *Philadelphia*'s depiction of Andy's depression after failing to secure a lawyer; as well as the chaotic, antisocial events in *Crazy Mama* and *Fighting Mad*. This sense of melancholy or despair is one over which most of Demme's characters triumph, a quality that makes *Crazy Mama*'s resolution all the more depressing, since in it we witness a capitulation to some of capitalism's more sordid demands.

According to Frye, the anticomic society "represents social reality, the obstacles to our desires that we recognize in the world around us."[25] In Demme's work, this society assumes the form of *Caged Heat*'s prison (which reflects the outside world's repressions); the capitalist structures in *Crazy Mama*, *Fighting Mad*, and *Melvin and Howard*; the mirror image CB radio society in *Citizens Band*; the dark, subversive otherworld of *Last Embrace*'s secret agency; the absurdist, comically dark world of the gang in *Married to the Mob*; the alienated milieu of Lecter and Gumb in *Silence of the Lambs*; and the apparently intolerant law firm in *Philadelphia*. In all of these cases, we are presented with a central figure, conceived of as a force of enlightenment (who may nevertheless, like Clarice and Andy, not be without their own darkness), who moves the film toward a satisfying resolution.

Frye notes that "the action of comedy is intensely Freudian in shape: the erotic pleasure principle explodes underneath the social anxieties sitting on top of it and blows them sky-high. But in comedy we see a victory of the pleasure principle that Freud warns us not to look for in ordinary life."[26] This observation highlights the satisfying endings of the most successful Demme films. Nevertheless, before this resolution is reached, a situation of conflict must first ensue, which often takes the form of an identity crisis. Frye likens this "period of confusion and sexual license"[27] (a phrase that immediately calls to mind the dissembling and dalliance of Charlie and Audrey early in *Something Wild*) to the "wood of no names that Alice passed through on her journey from pawn to queen,"[28] an interesting comparison that calls to mind the wood in which all of the major characters of *Citizens Band* wander looking for Floyd, who ultimately comes to represent the misplaced identity of the town of Unity, which, despite its name, has lost its sense of the communal.[29]

For some characters in Demme's films, though, there is no deliverance from contrariety and conflict. These characters (as with most characters at the beginning of a comedy) are similar to those whom Frye describes as "tyrannized over by some trait . . . that makes [the character] repeat a certain line of conduct mechanically"[30]—a description reminiscent of the loops of obsessive behavior in which Ray, Gumb, and the extended family in *Crazy Mama* find themselves, and from which they often are not capable of being delivered outside of the character's death.

Demme's work unites two essential literary techniques: the use of the alienated character or situation as a motivator of action, and the use of violence that is resolved in comic fashion. The director not only incorporates both of these strains into virtually all of his films, but also allows for the kinds of fictive conclusions involving renewal and hope that exemplify the true mythos of comedy.

Demme's films repeatedly exemplify a statement that occurs in both *Something Wild* and *Married to the Mob*: "what goes around comes around."[31] Characters' actions determine what subsequently happens to them, if not in a causal then certainly in a karmic way. There is a structural analogue to this belief; it can be referred to as the Demme ellipsis. Many of Demme's films, for example *Crazy Mama* (which starts in, and returns to, Jerusalem, Arkansas) and *Melvin and Howard* (which begins and ends with Melvin's drive in the desert), finish where they began. In *Something Wild*, this structure is used to its greatest effect. Not only does the film begin and end at the cafe; what we also see is horror being found at the periphery of Charlie and Audrey's journey and being brought back home to the suburbs. The repeated invocation of this pattern hints at an interaction between what happens in the physical and moral realms, suggesting that for

Demme the universe is in balance, and that individuals who upset that balance will eventually be equitably dealt with. The hope for the rest of us is that if we act in a moral way—if, in the words of *Married to the Mob*'s Angela, we "live a good life, a life we can be proud of"—we will somehow be rewarded. In the face of the often chaotic actions that Demme's films depict, this innocent, trusting belief in justice characterizes the films as paradigms of faith on which we can base our lives.

1 | Canned Heat

Demme's first directorial effort, *Caged Heat* (1974),[1] has to be approached with a number of facts in mind. We should recall that at the time of the film's production, Demme was working for Roger Corman, and that the assignments that Corman was giving to writers and directors like Demme were meant to be turned into films that very likely would play as part of a low-rental double feature package (the film itself cost only $180,000). Moreover, many of these films were intended for exhibition at drive-ins. Consequently, the films had to be fast moving, full of action, and redolent with a fair amount of either sexual suggestiveness or outright nudity. As director Jonathan Kaplan, who also worked for Corman, observed in a statement that could serve as a comment on many Demme/Corman films,

> There was a male sexual fantasy to be exploited, comedic subplot, action/violence, and a slightly-to-the-left-of-center subplot. Those were the four elements that were required in the nurses' pictures. And then frontal nudity from the waist up and total nudity from behind and no pubic hair and get the title of the picture somewhere into the film and go to work. And that was essentially it.[2]

In their apprentice films for Corman, *Angels Hard as They Come* (which Demme says is very loosely based on *Rashomon*) and *The Hot Box*, cowriter Joe Viola and Demme gave the audience what it wanted. In *Angels*, the use of motorcycle gangs—who for the teenage and drive-in audience were associated with fast action, excessive use of drugs, and exaggerated sexual appetites—proved to be a successful draw.[3] In *The Hot Box*, the nurses repeatedly either bathe in the nude or remove their blouses, all the time discussing left-wing politics and the rights of the proletariat. Especially in this film, Viola and Demme tried to stretch the boundaries of the exploitation genre by using a plot involving social consciousness and political sensitivity, concerns that have stayed with Demme to this day.

Caged Heat was the first film in which Demme was on his own, doing both the writing and directing. Demme's self-admitted difficulty in writing dialogue[4] might have been a drawback in a more demanding format, but here, in a somewhat formulaic women's prison picture, Demme is aided by the fact that the genre brings with it so many ideas concerning oppression and sexual exploitation that he has a firm base on which to structure his film. Previous women's prison films such as *Caged* had already made audiences familiar with the type of film in which women, placed in disadvantageous circumstances (mostly through the machinations of men, many of whom had framed them), band together against repressive prison forces. Indeed, *Caged* featured as a central character an innocent young woman very similar to *Caged Heat*'s Jacqueline Wilson (Erica Gavin). Like Eleanor Parker's Marie Wilson in *Caged*, *Caged Heat*'s Wilson is involved with a man found guilty of a crime in which the woman was only an accessory. Also like Marie, Jacqueline Wilson matures fairly quickly in prison in order to survive. The difference between the two films, though, is instructive. In *Caged*, the central character's education in crime as a means of survival is depicted as a sign of the failure of the penal system to prevent criminal indoctrination. In *Caged Heat*, Wilson's education in criminal behavior occurs along with her discovery that women are an oppressed class imprisoned by biased sexual attitudes.

What we have in the prison world of *Caged Heat* is nothing less than a microcosmic representation of the prejudices of the society on the outside. The irony in the film is that given the inmates' responsibility toward one another (this despite their occasional protests to the contrary), these women are actually superior to the members of the larger society who, it is implied, are for the most part ruthless and amoral. In rebelling against the prison system, then, *Caged Heat*'s inmates, who come to represent all women, rise above the corruptions of the male-dominated society that has had the audacity to judge them.

The prison situation is a desperate one in which death is always on the periphery of events. *Caged Heat*'s pre-title sequence shows us an undercover policeman approaching a house where a drug bust is about to take place. Three people quickly run out of the house before the policeman can enter it. The first one, played by Peter Fonda, gets away; the second is shot. Jacqueline Wilson, who in slowing down to help her wounded friend demonstrates her concern for others (a quality to which Demme will repeatedly draw attention in the film), is apprehended. Judged guilty of being an accessory to the "bodily assault of a police officer" and possession of dangerous drugs, she is sent to prison. The fact that in the courtroom sequence, except for the cut-away to the judge's gavel, all that we see is Wilson, and all that we hear is the judge's disembodied voice (an example of Demme's ability to turn a low budget to his favor), accentuates the impersonality and coldness of the judicial system, while the scene's darkness suggests the hopelessness and isolation into which Wilson is being thrust.

The routine degradation of the inmates begins on their arrival. Brought into the prison, the women are told to undress for a strip search by the prison physician, Dr. Randall (Warren Miller), who in spite of the fact that he is humming to himself quite pleasurably, says, "I don't enjoy this ritual any more than you do." Then, to accentuate the ludicrousness of this claim, as well as to underscore the outra-geousness of a male doctor's being allowed to perform a strip search on women, Demme has the doctor say that he is going to have the women do some calisthenics. "I'd like you girls to help me. We're go-ing to start off with some deep knee bends for openers," the doctor says, at which point Demme cuts to a low angle shot of the doctor putting on a rubber glove. The pun on "openers," with the implica-tion that the doctor is going to be probing these women's orifices, is bad enough; the reference to deep knee bends, which will allow the doctor to do vaginal and rectal searches for what he has already re-ferred to as the unusual things that you find inside of new arrivals, is especially ironic.

At the beginning of *Caged Heat*'s bawdy vaudeville show, we get the first glimpse of the prison superintendent, McQueen, who is ini-tially seen as an ominous shadow on the wall. Played by Barbara Steele (a vivacious and popular actress of the time whose most memorable work has been in horror films), McQueen is a young woman with horn-rimmed glasses; she is seated in a motorized wheelchair. There is a shawl over her legs, her hair is tightly bound to her head in an ex-tremely restrained manner, and there is a grim look on her face. It's clear that despite the fact that the prison's major authority figure is female, what we're dealing with is a daisy chain of alienation passed along to the prisoners, since McQueen's whole manner suggests that she has sublimated her natural impulses and has either been negatively influenced by, or has internalized, male views concerning the subju-gation of women (later, after someone tells a joke about sex, McQueen rubs her hands across her quilt and tightens her hands into fists in a fine representation of repressed desires). Appropriately, McQueen is followed into the auditorium by her secretary (whose style of dress makes her look like her boss's double) and the doctor, whose entrance, like the superintendent's and her secretary's, is anticipated by his shadow, a traditional symbol of death. Affecting a medical and ethical purity of purpose to which he has no legitimate claim, the doctor is dressed all in white. In a representation of his regressive attitudes, he is sucking on his pipe as though it were a bottle with a nipple (indeed, the doctor repeats this gesture, along with loud sucking noises, throughout the film). Together, the three characters seem like a trio out of a woman's worst nightmare about repression.

The vaudeville show put on by Belle (Roberta Collins) and Pandora (Ella Reid) is, predictably, risqué, yet it is also highly revealing since the whole show is a parody of traditional male attitudes toward women. Both women are dressed as men. Pandora says, "Hello, Bill, how are you tonight?," to which Belle replies, "Unbelievable, George; I feel just like a fighting cock," at which point she grabs her groin. In an aside to the audience, Pandora comments, "He looks more like a quarrelsome pecker to me." Despite the comedy, the point is well-taken. Belle mimics the strutting aggressiveness of a typical braggart male, shifting her weight down, thrusting her hips forward, and grabbing her "penis" as though the mere possession of this member were an accomplishment. At this point, Demme cuts away to the three main symbols of authority, McQueen, the doctor, and McQueen's secretary, who respectively cover their eyes, mouth, and ears—three state-paid monkeys aping the repressive, supposedly easily offended ethical attitudes of their society, and feigning an innocence that, given their aggressive and manipulative actions against the women whom they have trapped in the prison, they never exhibit.

After the show, when McQueen goes back to her office, the camera in a slow pan takes in its details. The office's walls are made out of soundproofing material, a symbol of McQueen's desire to be incognizant of the world outside of the narrowly limited one that she has constructed for herself. There is a framed photograph on the wall showing a mother, father, and two children (a boy and a girl) standing under a tree. Perhaps it is the superintendent's family. In any case, the way that the family is standing off-center in the photo makes it seem somewhat unbalanced (possibly suggesting psychological problems within the family group). After getting out of her wheelchair, McQueen lies down, undoes her collar, and takes off her glasses, actions signifying through the more relaxed physical attitude, loosening of clothing, and removal of accessories a slackening in the superintendent's self-repressive aspect that is mirrored in her dream.

McQueen's dream is her own personal vaudeville show, with herself as the star. As in the film's earlier dreams (Lavelle [Rainbeaux

Smith] and Jacqueline had also had one), sex takes center stage. The superintendent is dressed in a silver-lamé suit, with mesh stockings, high-heeled red shoes, and long black gloves. Her dark hair is loose, revealing its luster, and there's a black top hat on her head. Addressing an overflow audience of extremely responsive and appreciative inmates, McQueen says, "Don't you realize it was sex that put you behind bars in the first place?" It's an interesting question, since sex could apply both to the act of intercourse as well as to the male sex, which makes women targets of aggression.

The superintendent continues: "Stealing, to dress better for a man. Fornicating, packing the pockets of women-using pimps." Standing in front of lavatory doors, gateways behind which activities even more private than sex take place, the superintendent goes on with her litany of degrading female behavior, referring to acts involving the elimination of a sexual rival. "Give me contrition," she then says. "Let's have some redemption, repentance, repentance." Yet the dream, for all of its perceptiveness regarding the oppressive, paternalistic nature of corrupt heterosexual relationships and the institution that the superintendent serves, leaves McQueen's behavior unchanged. Unlike her inmates, the superintendent fails to draw a connection between the truths that her subconscious communicates and the material world in which she is operating. Thus, the next day, with her secretary taping every supposedly portentous word, the superintendent tells Belle and Pandora, "that show of yours last night was positively disgusting. Given a chance to express yourselves, you went straight to the gutter. Even for criminals you're just a particularly poor reflection on womanhood."

Yet McQueen reveals more than she intends. Belle and Pandora *did* go "straight to the gutter" with their show, but not in a pejorative sense. They went to the streets, where the unbalanced power relationships in society manifest themselves in the most undiluted way (later, the superintendent will distinguish among the prisoners on the basis of another power relationship, class, telling Wilson that because of her background she's different from the other women in the prison). And rather than being "a poor reflection on womanhood," Belle and Pandora's show presented an accurate critique of a certain kind of masculinity. Unfortunately, McQueen apparently regards her dream as little more than an aberrant vision; she cannot, or will not, see Belle and Pandora's show as a corollary to what she saw while asleep.

When she asks who wrote the show and gets no satisfactory answer, the superintendent holds out a picture taken from Pandora's cell and says that it suggests deviance, even though the photo is nothing more than a full frontal shot of a naked man, hardly a particularly inflammatory image. And yet after Belle and Pandora leave, McQueen, perhaps inspired by the photo, finds it impossible to deny her dream's significance. Confiding in her secretary, she says, "I had the strangest, most disturbing dream last night." When her aide begins to look interested, the superintendent continues, "Disturbing but [Demme here cuts away to show the aide's skeptical look] oddly gratifying." The superintendent allows herself a smile—the only spontaneous reaction she has in the entire film—and a bit of a laugh, then sucks in her cheeks to wipe off the smile, and looks down to go back to her work. She will not let the reality that the dream represents become a part of her waking consciousness.

In a subsequent scene, Maggie escapes during some field work, steals a truck, picks up Wilson on the way and, in a dizzying barrage of bullets, none of which seems to hit either of them, makes her escape. The pair stops at a service station, where Maggie aggressively berates a young male gas station attendant. In the meantime, while the man takes care of their car, Maggie and Wilson reveal important data about themselves to each other.

Maggie: You can handle yourself pretty good.
Wilson: So can you.
Maggie: I've had all the best teachers, babe. No way I was gonna flip out like those other weaklings. [To the attendant: Hurry it up, would ya?] So I decided to be just like the strongest person I know: Jack, the prick that railroaded me in the first place.
Wilson: Sounds like quite a guy.
Maggie: We robbed a million banks together. Never the same city twice. . . . It's easy if you got a gun and know how to move fast. Yeah, we really had it down. I never got caught, except once, thanks to that pair of all Jacks.

The irony of Maggie's statement is striking. She contrasts herself with the other inmates by calling them weaklings, even though all of the women (herself included) are victims of the same social forces. And despite her supposedly well-informed stance, Maggie still models herself on a most unfortunate individual: an ex-boyfriend, whom she at once lauds ("the strongest person") and criticizes ("the prick that . . ."), thereby revealing not only her ambiguous attitude toward this man but also unwittingly drawing attention to the stupidity of her adulation. When Maggie says that she "never got caught, except once," she demonstrates that she fails to realize that getting caught once is more than enough. Maggie has apparently forgotten the lesson that she seemed to have learned while in prison: that she was there because of men, and that the behavior patterns of many men (male criminals among them) involve manipulation and deception. Maggie's desire for her reprehensible ex-boyfriend reveals her poor self-image at the same time as it also shows us how trapped she is by social conditioning, which encourages her to yield to men as the only way to gain a modicum of power.

Meanwhile, in a complementary scene, McQueen is coquettishly talking with the doctor, playing up to him in a terribly sycophantic way by affecting the role of an innocent little girl, thereby exhibiting in exaggerated form one of the most demeaning kinds of behavior that American society encourages in women.

> You know, Doctor, there's so many things about modern technology that I don't understand. Things that must be crystal clear to a man of science like yourself. Rockets to the moon, correcting human behavior with drugs and surgery. I don't know; perhaps I'm just old-fashioned.

Becoming coy, and then catching herself in the act of being flirtatious, McQueen looks over at her aide and, noticing the tape recorder used to record all of her statements to the inmates, and not wanting to have revealed for the record how her poor self-image has resulted in her acting subserviently (significantly, she does so with the only male in the prison, thereby revealing how illusory her power in the institution is), she asks, "That thing's not on, is it?"

In the meantime, Wilson and Pandora have secretly returned to the prison to liberate Belle, who has been scheduled for a lobotomy. With McQueen and her assistant and the doctor in tow, the women make their escape; they are last seen heading over a ridge and disappearing as Demme cuts to a point-of-view shot of a rolling landscape, which, presumably, is seen out of the window of the getaway car.

Despite the film's social critiques, the viewer of *Caged Heat* should realize that its characterizations are skewed; none of the prisoners seems to be hostile or malicious without reason. And of those whose backgrounds are supplied, none seems to have committed any serious crime—that is, no serious crime that was committed without very substantial justification (Pandora's claim to have cut off a man's

Wilson holding a shotgun on the doctor during the liberation of Belle

testicles doesn't seem seriously offered). In league with the film's exaggerated stylistics (e.g., stretch printing and asynchronous sound), this method of romantic, hyperbolic characterization tells us that Demme is more interested in the idea of prison as a metaphor for repression than in the depiction of an actual prison itself (the fantasy sequences certainly underscore this point).

As in *Married to the Mob*, *Caged Heat*'s excesses create a fabulous world in which violence does not have the same impact as in a more traditional fiction. Even when graphic violence takes place—as when an officer's ear gets shot off—we tend to feel somewhat distanced from the event by virtue of the freewheeling tone that Demme has adopted. This effect can work against the film, though. When we see the doctor preparing for Belle's psychosurgery by picking up a conventional power drill, we're encouraged by dint of this absurdity to treat the whole sequence as less than serious, even the parts in which the doctor sexually molests the anesthetized Belle. Demme needed here to strike a balance between a fanciful and a realistic approach, perhaps by emphasizing the scene's dramatic aspects so as to avoid undercutting its potential impact.

To an extent, *Caged Heat*'s female nudity, which is predominantly gratuitous, also compromises its social message. For a film whose major theme is female subjugation to resort to borderline exploitation (as

Demme also does in *The Silence of the Lambs*) is unfortunate. Never-theless, at *Caged Heat*'s end, what we hope for is that Belle, Pandora, and Wilson, now free of the prison's confines, will somehow also be free of the ignorance that put them in prison in the first place. It's a wish for the kind of deliverance from oppression that will be the the-matic concern of all subsequent Demme films.

2 | Road Crazies

While somewhat lackluster and disjointed, *Crazy Mama* (1975) is nonetheless an interesting work in that, as a road movie about a dispossessed family, it functions as a precursor for ideas about figurative journeys and family structure that will emerge more fully developed in later films such as *Melvin and Howard* and *Something Wild*.

Part of *Crazy Mama*'s weakness doubtless stems from the fact that Demme was given the project only ten days before shooting started when Shirley Clark, the original director, and producer Roger Corman had a disagreement that ended Clark's participation in the film. Several parts had yet to be cast and the script needed to be rewritten—additional responsibilities that fell to Demme. Yet even so, Corman seems to have felt that Demme could have done a better job. As Demme recalls: "Roger beat me over the head about not getting enough warmth into the characters. He hated my second movie, *Crazy Mama*, hated it to the degree that he almost didn't let me direct *Fighting Mad*."[1]

Crazy Mama's family is by no means a traditional one. Rather, this is a family that starts out whole, is fragmented, and is then rebuilt in a way that results in a strange mixture of chaos and compassion that is a hallmark of Demme's work. Of course, there are fragmented families in other Demme films. Melvin Dummar's wife Lynda keeps leaving him because he isn't the stable provider she desires; the family of *Something Wild*'s Charlie Driggs broke up before the film began (Charlie's wife left with the family dentist); the husband of *Married to the Mob*'s Angela de Marco is murdered early in the film. In each case, though, fate eventually steps in to give the central characters another chance at some form of familial integration. It's almost as if Demme is saying that we need bad things to happen to us so that we may learn from these experiences, and that if we do learn, the universe grants us a second opportunity for happiness.

Demme encourages us toward a family structure that is tolerant, loving, and self-supporting, qualities that represent an extension of traditional democratic values. The director seems to believe in families in which everyone has an equal voice—and he moves us toward an appreciation of these families through his films' acceptance of the crazy-quilt way that many innovative family structures are created (which itself mirrors the manner in which the structure of real American families has mutated since the nuclear model of the 1960s). In *Crazy Mama*, what we see is an entirely new family built up out of old boyfriends and people whom one just meets along the way. And although the film doesn't concentrate exclusively on the idea of family (it contains a great deal of poorly justified murder and mayhem), the accent on family is nonetheless always there in the background as a kind of thematic constant that emerges as the film's most important feature.

Crazy Mama starts in Jerusalem, Arkansas, in 1932, during the Great Depression, and shows Daniel Stokes killed while defending his family farm against repossession by the local bankers, who arrive with the sheriff as reinforcement. Although the scene is shot in a gauzy haze that suggests a lost Edenic innocence, the action is neither pleasant nor romanticized. In the film's next sequence, it's 1958; Stokes's widow, Sheba (Ann Sothern), and daughter, Melba (Cloris Leachman), who are running a beauty parlor in California (the promised land of *The Grapes of Wrath*'s Joad family), are similarly behind in their payments, so they're evicted from their business. After a car chase with a debtor (whose Cadillac they steal, the first example in the film of the attitude that theft may be the only way in capitalist America for the disenfranchised to assert some form of power), Melba decides to take the family (which includes her teenaged daughter and her daughter's two boyfriends) back to reclaim their farm in Jerusalem in a redemptive journey reminiscent of the one taken by the Jews led by Moses. (Apparently, Melba believes that since California has been a failure, a return to the family's original promised land will save them.) Along the way they stop off in that Mecca of capitalism, Las Vegas, where they pick up a septuagenarian woman, Bertha (Merle Earle), and Joe Bob (Stewart Granger), a wealthy man who becomes attracted to Melba. The rest of the film is one robbery after another, each one followed by car chases, gun battles, and close-call getaways.

As in *Caged Heat*, *Crazy Mama*'s plot is just a throwaway, although it is more of an annoyance here than anything else. Fortunately, Demme invests the film with diverting bits of Americana (which he views as evidence of the good humor that might redeem

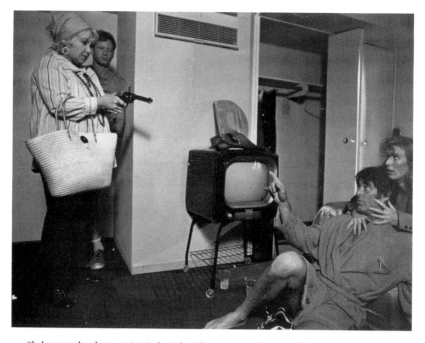

Sheba gets the drop on Joe Bob and Melba in a Las Vegas motel room

the country), from Burma Shave signs ("She put a bullet / through his hat / but he's had / closer shaves than that / Burma Shave"), to a motel that is a series of concrete tepees, to comic non sequiturs (during a television news show that is a classic of technical ineptitude, Joe Bob's wife says that her "husband is a married man").

A speech by Bertha indicates why she feels so secure with the rag-tag bunch that has been transformed into the extended Stokes family: "I ain't been so free since I broke out of the old folks home. That step-son of mine, the bastard (he was the last kin I had left), decided to put me away. That was seven years ago. Today is my seventy-fifth birthday. . . . It's the first time for seventeen years I haven't been alone for my birthday. I feel like I have my family again."

Demme is celebrating the bonding and unity among these people. Unfortunately, these celebrations occupy very little time in the film. Moreover, the plot device that propels the film doesn't make much sense. *Crazy Mama* never follows through on its case for social injustice being visited on the Stokes family regarding the loss of their farm. It's not John Stokes with whom the film is concerned but his heirs, and their only fault seems to be that, like Melvin Dummar, they're bad at handling money. Unlike the outlaw characters in Arthur Penn's *Bonnie and Clyde*, the Stokes family members aren't shown sympathizing with other unfortunates like themselves. Without an underlying rationale for their behavior, which could have been present if the social injustice theme of the film's beginning had been retained, the "family" seems more like a collection of malcontents than anything else. Lacking the social and sexual critique of *Caged Heat*, *Crazy Mama* stands as little more than an excuse for a series of wild actions and car chases.

What almost redeems *Crazy Mama* is a notion implied by its story. The film traces a road journey that starts out in one location only to return to it (the film's final shot, which does not constitute part of its main action, takes place in Florida). The way that *Crazy Mama* doubles back onto itself does more than return the characters to Jerusalem, Arkansas; it also throws the audience back onto Demme's ellipsis of karma, which here demonstrates that battling the prevailing social system by mimicking or appropriating its excessive behaviors (like stealing, an activity in which the Stokes "family" engages) is, in the end, an exercise in futility (in this respect, the film is very similar to *Fighting Mad*). Moreover, the mistake that the "family" makes is to fail to see that staying within the system as entrepreneurs (who don't in any case seem particularly well organized), and then going on from there to believe that robbing banks will somehow solve their problems, highlights their lack of insight and ingenuity in confronting the way that the capitalist system works.

Indeed, the fact that the "family" drifts toward Las Vegas, where, as Sheba and Bertha realize, the odds are wildly stacked against you (as in any capitalist enterprise), underscores their mistaken trust in the force of money as a source of pleasure (a notion complemented by Demme's having the song "Money," with its bitterly materialistic lyrics like "Money can't buy everything it's true / What it can't buy I can't use," playing on the soundtrack). This is clear as well from the way that, in an attempt to pray for winnings, Sheba and Bertha mouth homilies like "God Bless America" and "Remember the Alamo" while at the slot machines. As Bertha says, "You have to be in close contact with the deity to make these machines pay, and you have to believe in America," making it plain that for her (and the rest of the "family" as well), money is the all-American god. It is a tragic testimony to these people's shortsightedness that unlike other Demme characters who drop out of conventional culture to seek more positive, alternative lifestyles, the characters in *Crazy Mama* decide to go up against American culture on its own terms in a fight that is far less noble than foolhardy.

As *Crazy Mama*'s conclusion makes plain, though, despite their long and arduous road journey, none of the Stokes "family" (in contrast to similar road travelers like *Something Wild*'s Charlie and Audrey) have learned a thing. Bertha is shot trying to collect some ransom money; Sheba and Joe Bob die during two of the film's pointless shootouts. Melba, her daughter Cheryl (Linda Purl), and Cheryl's two suitors, Sean (Donn Most), and Snake (Bryan Englund)—all suitably disguised by changed hair colors and styles—are last seen working within the symbolically cramped confines of yet another two-bit business: a hamburger stand. In the action under the end credits, Melba doles out food while, in a final and regrettable return to the film's beginning (in *Crazy Mama*, the Demme ellipsis has decidedly depressing results), the perennial creditor comes for his money. That last great big dollar bill that seemingly sticks to the camera lens at the film's end is there to tell us that only when we get away from regarding money as the highest form of achievement are we ever going to be truly able to improve ourselves as a nation. Until that time, Mama, you'd have to be crazy to believe in such a corrupt and disorderly system.

Like *Crazy Mama*, *Fighting Mad* (1976) is a film about getting back one's rights. The difference here is that in the time between the two productions, Demme sharpened his directorial skills sufficiently to avoid incredible and boring actions.

Although he is once again working within the framework of a Roger Corman exploitation vehicle, Demme manages to find the perfect format for expressing his belief in progressive libertarian values versus those of entrenched and reactionary social forces. The result is that while on a realistic level the film is somewhat absurd, on an emotional level it is eminently satisfying.[2]

As in the classic romance, in *Fighting Mad* there is virtually no middle ground between good and evil. Unrealistic though it may be, this type of structure satisfies the audience's desire to see justice carried out, something that doesn't often happen in the "real" world. The appeal of *Fighting Mad*, which Demme wrote, stems from the fact that it appropriates the exaggerations inherent in Corman's style of filmmaking and legitimizes them by invoking romance.

Most of Corman's films take as their subject matter either horror or social fringe groups; monsters appear in the first category of films, outcasts such as motorcycle bikers and criminals in the second. In either category, clear oppositions are set up between classes of characters: the law-abiding citizens, all of whom are very normal (to the extent that the Corman style allowed them to be), are on one side; the outsiders who threaten the prevailing social order—no matter what type of misfits they are, monsters or motorcyclists—are on the other.

Fighting Mad goes beyond this paradigm by retaining the aspect of divisiveness but also collapsing the roles of the law-abider and the outsider. Here, the protagonist is a rebel who serves a law higher than the one represented by conventional law enforcement agencies. Demme also adapts the format by making the villain with whom the rebel contends a representative (albeit a caricatured one) of the capitalist class. Pierce Crabtree (a tag name suggesting a rape of the natural world) is a land developer, a man eager to appropriate and corrupt the virgin land for exploitative purposes.

Fighting Mad is thus really nothing more than an updated western, a basic morality play, with the Peter Fonda character as the lone rider for justice and Crabtree as an example of the Old West banker who was ready to purchase or finance the land that had been discovered and fought for by the pioneers. Demme even goes so far as to incorporate into the film Peter Fonda's penchant for motorcycles, machines that bring along with them connotations of the rebel, an association that the Corman studio had built up in films like *Hell's Angels on Wheels* and *Angels Hard as They Come* (the latter of which starred Fonda and featured a script cowritten by Demme). Indeed, in the way that it shows the corrupt characters in the film driving MGs and Cadillacs, while the morally upright characters either drive more proletarian vehicles or motorcycles (Fonda's father rides a motorcycle; the honest judge in the film, who is also classed as an outsider by being referred to as "a health nut," rides a bike), *Fighting Mad* assigns symbolic importance to the type of transportation that one uses.

Fonda's character, Tom Hunter, whose name connotes a natural activity, has been in trouble before; he is always fighting mad when he sees injustice, with which he comes in contact right from the film's beginning. Demme is careful to characterize the two sides in the film's conflict very early. Male construction workers are seen harassing a woman on the street; others bother a young, long-haired man. Hunter comes to this man's aid after first tucking his wire-rimmed glasses into his shirt pocket, a characterizing gesture that Tom will use throughout the film. (Later, we realize that the construction men, with their atavistic values, are doubtless working for Crabtree Enterprises).

The achievement of vengeance may seem attractive within the context of the film's fiction, but it is nonetheless a highly objectionable form of behavior. One has only to point to the fact that all we see in *Fighting Mad* is one murder giving rise to another to realize how dangerous this kind of activity can be. This pattern is objected to by Tom's father, who knows that despite its attractiveness, fighting for change by waging one small battle at a time is futile, since it doesn't

Peter Fonda in *Fighting Mad*

involve the implementation of a clearly defined program of action, which, it is implied, is what is needed to bring about meaningful progress.

Demme gives Tom's father a speech about the need for wide open spaces, which, along with the old man's association with horses, tells us that the values he represents are those of the Old West pioneer. Although the speech includes a reference to changing times that sounds reminiscent of something Pat Garrett says in Sam Peckinpah's *Pat Garrett and Billy the Kid* ("Times changing, Billy"), the fact is that the forces working against development of rural areas seem destined to fail given people's desires for conveniently available goods and services. That's why the resolution of the final shootout at *Fighting Mad's* end seems so unsatisfying: all of Tom's struggle seems for nought. Armed first with the more traditional weaponry of a hunter, a bow and arrow, Tom, creeping around Crabtree's estate, disables two of Crabtree's men, thus defeating their advanced technology by using a more elementary approach. Then, in contrast to the thugs' high-powered infrared scope rifles, Tom, using a conventional gun, kills the rest of Crabtree's goons and finally, in a just payback for Crabtree's responsibility for the death of Tom's father, shoots Crabtree himself.

Riddled with at least four bullets, Tom is placed into an ambulance; given his serious condition, one wouldn't expect him to survive. What, then, are we to make of the film's last scene, which is bathed in golden light, and which shows Tom and his son walking back from a fishing excursion? Within the film's fictive reality, is this shot real or, given the overtly romantic lighting, imaginary—a hoped-for future that is never to be? Demme leaves this issue unresolved, and maybe his film is the better for it. At *Fighting Mad*'s conclusion, Demme seems to be saying that, given our desire to see the good guys win, and the difficulty of reconciling this desire with the "real world," the best that we can hope for is a fairy tale ending. Until Demme reaches greater sophistication in bringing together exaggerated action and the empirical world, as he does in *Something Wild* and *Married to the Mob*, that kind of resolution will have to be enough to satisfy us.

3 | Radio Daze

At the height of the CB radio craze, Jonathan Demme took Paul Brickman's script for *Citizens Band*[1] and made a delightful film out of the notion that citizens band communication is an ideal metaphor for people's desire to communicate in many different ways. The fact that Demme simultaneously shows a great deal of affection for the characters whom he so very gently satirizes not only makes *Citizens Band* (1977) a pleasure to watch but also qualifies the film as the purest expression of Demme's ethic concerning the need of each individual to feel that he or she is part of something more significant than one's self. *Citizens Band* is thus a comic film with a serious democratic premise: that in terms of voice (and, one hopes, behavior as well), everyone should have an equal say in what happens in his or her community/nation.

Although *Citizens Band* was well received critically (the film was chosen as the year's best by the National Society of Film Critics), it nonetheless did poorly at the box office. Apparently, *Citizens Band* was released without audience testing in order to capitalize quickly on the CB craze—an unfortunate miscalculation. Demme has said that the film's financial failure was so great as to make it impossible for him to get work for a time.[2]

Citizens Band simultaneously tracks a number of stories, all of them centered on conflicts associated with love: those involving Blaine, a good-natured CB devotee who is known in citizens band circles as Spider (played by Paul Le Mat in his first turn as one of Demme's upright young men), his gym teacher brother Dean (Bruce McGill), and the woman with whom both brothers are romantically involved, Pam (Candy Clark). The brothers also have a complicated emotional relationship with their crotchety father, Floyd (Roberts Blossom). Contrasted to the romantic triangle controlled by Pam is one dominated by truck driver Harold (Charles Napier), whose bigamy is exposed when his two wives both show up to nurse him after he runs his rig into a ditch. Additionally, there are conflicts created by the people spuriously using the CB airwaves, especially the emergency channel, which is needed three times in the film. Blaine's anger over the misuse of this channel makes us more aware of his contention that serious communication, on an emergency basis or not, is of paramount concern.

Much of the film's sexually based conflict is in evidence right from *Citizens Band*'s beginning, when the mysterious voice of Electra (who, it turns out, is really Pam) is heard, followed by the radio airwaves sex that she has with a young man whose CB "handle" (i.e., his assumed name) is Warlock (Will Seltzer). This use of the citizens band seems somewhat curious, though; one would think that sexual relations would be bringing people together when, in fact, the film demonstrates that quite often, the opposite is the case—that people don't want the commitment that is an adjunct of sex so much as they simply want some form of spurious intimacy that does not involve human contact. In this sense, *Citizens Band* prefigures the phenomenon of telephone sex, which in the 1990s has mushroomed into a million-dollar-a-year business that represents a sad mixture of the need for love and the inability to directly express it.

The "sex" between Electra and Warlock is characterized by disembodied voices linking up electronically, with the additional consideration that although Warlock is being titillated, Electra is doubtless only faking her responses. Pam later justifies her actions by saying that Blaine told her to "have fun" with the radio and, as Electra, perhaps that's what she thinks she is doing, but she's having fun at the expense of someone else's serious romantic and sexual interest in her. The degree of manipulation and control that she exhibits is objectionable, although it is saved from total condemnation by the fact that it comically inverts the conventional situation in which it is the male who is casual about sex and the woman who is intimately involved.

The irony here, of course, is that instead of bringing people together, the way that the citizens band is commonly used tends to keep these people apart (Warlock never asks to meet Electra in person). People use their CBs to mask their identities: a young boy pretends to be a hustler, Pam plays the part of a seducer, Dean takes the name of Blood to vent his hostility against his brother, and Floyd expresses all of his sadness and alienation only to his radio buddies, never to either one of his sons. Indeed, Blaine and Dean have their own problems

Pam and Blaine on the air in *Citizens Band*

with communication, most of them centering on their relations with Pam, who wants a directness and intimacy from each of them that they find it quite difficult to give her.

However, toward the film's end (when Floyd disappears), the town's citizens drop their masks and start relating to one another forthrightly. Simultaneously, the emergency channel is finally used as Blaine conceives it is supposed to be: as a means of bringing the aptly named town of Union[3] together into a community of mutual feelings and trust that Demme conceives of as the true end of the democratic ideal (at the film's conclusion, *Citizens Band*'s title is inverted as the town of Union finally becomes a band of citizens). What *Citizens Band* seems to be saying, then, is that used properly, advanced electronics can actually bring us back to our real selves, just the opposite of the message in such anti-technology films as *The Conversation*,

Blow Up, and Brian De Palma's gloss on the previous two films, *Blow Out*, all of which use electronics as correlatives for the progressive alienation of people from one another.

The fact that *Citizens Band* is not only about radio but also about communication, the lack of which is the basis of all of the characters' problems, lends to the film a coherence that prevents it from seeming like a disordered collection of tales. This aspect gives Demme the freedom to move back and forth from one character's story to another's without threatening the film's coherence. At *Citizens Band*'s beginning, all of its stories are operating independently of each other, and then slowly coalesce. Early on, there are isolated examples of linkages in the film: Blaine saves Harold; Dean, Pam, and Blaine are associated through their use of the radio; Blaine's campaign against misuse of the emergency channel brings him in touch with the preacher (Ed Begley, Jr.), who has boosted his CB's amplitude, effectively crowding alternative opinions off the airwaves in an example of electronically enhanced religious intolerance. However, all of these actions really only come together in the film's major event: the flight of Floyd, whose "handle" is Papa Thermodyne, and whose disappearance and rescue make it plain that when finally faced with an emergency that concerns one of their own, the whole town can work in concert (the fact that Floyd is seen riding one of Harold's lost cows at the film's end—indeed, he has found the entire herd, which had strayed away—only makes the unification of *Citizens Band*'s stories that much more satisfying).

The CBers, who usually hide behind the medium's electronic cloak (which involves the use of assumed names), finally act in the manner of Blaine/Spider, who, as his nickname suggests, sits at the center of a web (in this case, a web of separate story strands), beneficently feels along his web the vibrations of the characters' different struggles and desires, and (unwittingly) spins them all together at the end. Yet before this point, we see that none of the film's characters is able to successfully communicate. Despite the bilious pronouncements of the Aryan white supremacist (whose CB handle is "The Red Baron"), these people don't use the airwaves for power or revolt, as does Mark Hunter, the lead character in director Allan Moyle's *Pump Up the Volume*, a film about (illegal) radio transmitting that acts as a companion piece to Demme's film. However, like *Pump Up the Volume*'s Mark, *Citizens Band*'s people often only seem to come alive while on the air, and only come to terms with their real selves when their electronic persona is either destroyed or rejected because of their realizing the human consequences of their actions.

Unlike the film's approach to characterization, which initially emphasizes the things that people do and only then inquires into why they do them, *Citizens Band*'s first images start from the inside and work their way out. Under the film's credits, Demme shows us the internal electronics of CB radios, panning past and dissolving among wires, circuit boards, and so on, at the same time as we hear some of the disembodied voices that will eventually be attached to personalities in the film. One voice, which we subsequently learn is Electra's, says, "There are a lot of voices out there but yours is different; I like it. Come on." The latter phrase is CB lingo for an invitation to further communication, but in colloquial terms it also operates as a teasing request, in this case for some form of involvement. Another speaker is so obsessively concerned with his electronics that he seems to lose his self-confidence when they fail him. "Is there something wrong with my modulation? I just don't want to lose my modulation. Yesterday I lost my modulation and I was unhappy all day," he says. Another man precisely identifies the kind of transference that can take place when people communicate predominantly by voices only, without the assistance of visual contact and body gestures to reinforce meanings. "You don't sound too good—I mean not your radio but your voice," he says, placing the proper accent not on the possible failure of the electronics but on the sound of the speaker himself. Yet another voice identifies one of CB's problems: "How do you know if anyone's listening? . . . I just want someone to talk to." And when a final voice tries to tie down Electra's voice to some recognizable personality, asking, "Who are you, anyway?" Electra responds, "Wouldn't you like to know?" a statement to which the original speaker responds, "Yeah, me and nine other guys."

The situation with Electra is emblematic of the artificial kind of communication on the citizens band, as opposed to the way that Blaine uses it. Electra engages in electronic sex with Warlock that is doubly removed from reality because it involves a significant degree of fantasizing as well. When she asks Warlock, "Can we undo a few buttons," it's clear that Warlock must undo the buttons himself and can only pretend that Electra is somehow involved in this activity. (The fact that throughout her talk with Warlock, Electra is engaged in eating a sandwich shows just how disinterested she really is.) The objectionable aspect of Electra and Warlock's "sex" is exacerbated by the fact that Warlock got Electra's name from his best friend, Death Row, a name which suggests that both young men are condemned to a deadly life of loneliness without women, and by the lyric playing in Warlock's car: "I'm not in love, so don't forget it; it's just a silly phase I'm going through." Yet the Electra/Warlock conversation is certainly diverting—so much so, in fact, that Harold, who is listening to it, inadvertently becomes involved in an accident.

In the same way that, using electronics (telephones), Harold stays in contact with his wives, Connie (also known as Portland Angel [Marcia Rudd]) and Joyce (or Dallas Angel [Ann Wedgeworth]), and also manages to keep them apart, so too is electronics used to point up failed communication in the next scene, during which Blaine and his father sit down to breakfast, barely saying a word to each other.

Blaine: How ya feeling today, Pop?
Floyd: Okay.
Blaine: How'd ya sleep last night?
Floyd: Okay.

Yet when the CB sings out with a call for Floyd, he lights up with the heat that his CB name suggests.

The relationship between Blaine and Floyd is emotionally repressed, as is the relationship between Blaine and Dean, who is so obsessed with discipline that he won't let a gym student who needs to urinate leave the room. "[You] should've thought about that before class," he tells the boy. And although Demme employs a panning technique in the gym scene, having the camera follow one character and then pick up another later, thereby implying an intertwining of the characters' lives, *Citizens Band* at this point is still emphasizing alienation. When Blaine tells the kid to go to the bathroom, Dean becomes enraged. "This is my class; this is my gym. This is where I work. I do not need you disrupting things," he says. However, the slippage between Dean's statement and behavior is made clear when the gym door opens and Pam abruptly enters the room with her class, slamming the door loudly. Seeing that it's his girlfriend, Dean ignores the "disrupt[ion]" and reacts with pleasure.

In contrast to the way that most of *Citizens Band*'s other characters communicate, Debbie (Alix Elias), a prostitute who uses the "handle" Hot Coffee, is quite unaffected, and has a very straightforward (albeit illegitimate given Harold's being married) relationship with Harold, whom she has apparently known for years. In contrast to Electra's "come-on[s]," which are explicitly about sex but which never result in direct contact, all of Debbie's invitations are geared toward physical liaisons. And though Debbie's airwave statements must by necessity be somewhat metaphoric (she invites the truckers to have hot coffee, although they all know that she's the one who's "hot"), these meetings still have concrete results.

Harold and Debbie's relationship is not only direct, it is even comprehensive and accepting enough to allow discussion of Harold's two wives (although this doesn't change the fact that we still don't respect Harold very much). And like Blaine and Floyd when they discuss their breakfast cereal, Debbie and Harold simultaneously demonstrate their embracing of American values and the film's comic use of misdirected rhetoric. Here, instead of Electra's use of language to mislead people and protect herself, Harold and Debbie unwittingly encourage us to believe that they're talking about one thing while they're really discussing something entirely different. After they have sex, Harold (off-screen) says, "I been around a long time . . . but nobody makes it like you." We think he's talking about intercourse, but Debbie's response shows how wrong we are. "That's 'cause I grind my own beans," Debbie says, to which Harold replies, "It's just delicious." And to top off what is already a comic misunderstanding on our part, Debbie (like *Melvin and Howard*'s Melvin Dummar) can't seem to resist responding in terminology gleaned from television commercials. "It's part Colombian, part French Roast; that's what makes it creamy yet full-bodied," she says.

When Debbie complains that her business is falling off because, given the 55 mile-per-hour speed limit, "now nobody's got time for nothing" (an allusion that also embraces the American rush for satisfaction that has made it difficult for people to slow down and relate to one another), Harold decides to turn overt commercialism to good use by helping Debbie buy a mobile home so that she can "entertain" men right on the side of the road. Demme is careful not to spare us the motor home salesman's pitch, which refers to the fact that the model at which Harold and Debbie are looking "sleeps three standard with a 5/7 option available." In another example of comic misunderstanding, Debbie takes the salesman to mean that he's referring to a multiple *menage*. "Well, golly, that's plenty; I never even done three," she says. (Of course, the van is CB-equipped).

Harold makes a significant statement that only seems to be about the mobile home. "You know something, Debbie, it's a funny country. Everything's going mobile. Now if you can accept that, I mean if you could swing with it, you could do anything." The mobility Harold is referring to isn't just the physical kind, though; he's also (albeit unconsciously) talking about the easy transfer of affections and morals. It's not a very pretty state of affairs that he describes, encompassing people with no fixed abode and a lack of dependable values (thus his use of the phrase "swing with it," which at the time of the film's release must have called up images of "swingers," people who, married or not, had many different sexual partners). Yet for all of his duplicity and "swinging," Harold is also a fairly nice man. Making the down payment on Debbie's camper, Harold gives her as the reason for his action the fact that "the other day a guy [Blaine] saved my life; this'll about do it for you." Harold's gesture exemplifies Demme's belief in an ellipsis of good karma, that a good deed done for you makes it incumbent upon you to do something good for someone else.

Nevertheless, for all of these allusions to good will, *Citizens Band* hasn't brought us any closer to a suggestion of how the people of Union can directly communicate without somehow taking advantage of one another (we can't forget that for all of her good-heartedness, Debbie is still a prostitute and Harold is still a bigamist and an adulterer). After Harold's wives (who despite the differences in their personalities manage to communicate and commiserate right from the start) meet while taking the same bus to Union to comfort Harold, he tries to explain away his bigamy with a line that he has previously used on both of them ("When you've been on the road for a long time, you forget just how soft a woman really feels"). However, the statement is nothing more than a self-serving comment meant to deliver him from judgment. It's not a confession so much as a sales pitch to get him what he wants. `

Harold isn't the only character in the film who has forgotten how to express himself honestly. Most of *Citizens Band*'s characters don't know how to directly give vent to their emotions. The airwaves priest mouths phony God slogans; the Aryan is a textbook racist; Electra is all duplicitous sex talk; the old woman blathers incoherent memories; the "Hustler" is just a young kid. It's therefore ironic that given the emphasis on direct expressions of emotion, it is disaffection, not amity, that causes Dean and Pam to talk candidly. During one of the few times in the film that Demme uses a symbolic visual motif, Dean and Pam have a discussion in the deserted gym that shows us how conceptually far apart they really are, a state that Demme underscores by having them walk together in and out of shadows that suggest the dark, never-mentioned places in their relationship. When Dean reacts in a very hostile way to the news that his brother has visited Pam, she complains, "You're so competitive," thereby using his alliance with sports against him. By contrast, when, a little while later, Blaine and Pam are in the gym, the place of Dean's authority, Blaine tries to directly communicate to Pam his feelings for her, telling her that he's going to finally evidence the independence she wants him to have by leaving home.

Demme starts the scene in the gym with Jordan Cronenweth's camera about twenty feet away, shooting Blaine, who's on a practice horse, through a set of parallel bars that enclose him in a symbolic representation of his emotional limitations. After a group of cheerleaders leaves and Blaine and Pam have some privacy, Pam begins to show a progressive interest in what Blaine is saying, a state that Demme reflects by gradually moving his camera closer. When the camera is about three feet away, Demme employs the symbolic device of a shaft of light from above that filters down between the two characters, at once defining the still present distance between them but simultaneously emblematizing this rift in terms of a symbol of hope and communication that augurs well for the resolution of the couple's talk. Then, increasing the scene's significance by widening its realm to include Dean, Demme also shows us the linkage between the two locations where Dean and Blaine/Pam are situated as well as the psychological distance between them. Although Dean is outside of Blaine and Pam's realm of action (he is in the hall), he nonetheless sees them directly, looking at the couple through the window in the gym door. Dean sees but cannot touch or speak; Blaine and Pam see each other but do not see or hear Dean (it's almost as though Dean, like the listeners to Electra's radio encounters, overhears, but cannot physically participate in, the action).

As viewers, our inability to see anything more than a reflection of what Dean sees directly (we see Blaine and Pam's images in a mirror on the wall near Dean) tells us how, even as a relatively omniscient audience, we nonetheless can have our vision restricted, emphasizing that at best we can only really experience a pale reflection of what Dean must be going through. And though all of the scene's characters are present in the same frame, physically the two groups are as separated spatially as Dean must feel psychologically, alienated as he is from what he sees happening between his girlfriend and his brother, who are still in love with each other. The fact that the mirror shot also makes Blaine and Pam look smaller than Dean, who is standing close to the camera, doesn't diminish the couple for us so much as it reminds us that the most important emotions for Demme at this point are Dean's, who is experiencing a great deal of pain.

This scene marks *Citizens Band*'s midpoint, when the alienation between the film's characters is greatest, and after which it finally starts to diminish. First, the film's major symbol of alienation, the an-

Blaine, Pam, and Floyd at dinner. Is that really dog meat in the stew?

tenna belonging to the Aryan white supremacist, is torn down. Floyd tells Blaine one day that if he leaves the house, he will kill Blaine's dog, which is followed by the most beautiful shot in the whole film: Floyd, sitting outside in the sun with his CB radio, the dog placidly lying near him. Floyd is talking on the radio about his personal vision of peace, his return to Canada: "Mercy, that Canada's pretty country. All them cows. Mercy sakes, I've never seen such beauty in one place. Hey, good buddy, maybe some day we'll meet there and have a dog gone good time. How about that? Mercy, gracious."

On the word "gracious," Floyd breaks down and sobs. The sun shining, the dog near Floyd, and the outdoor scene, contrasted with the unhappy old man, result in an emotionally honest scene that helps us understand Floyd as we had not before.

That night, when Blaine brings Pam to dinner, the dog is gone, and it looks as though Floyd has made good on his previous threats and killed him. However, Pam sees through Floyd's ruse, even though Blaine doesn't. Unlike Floyd's two sons, Pam (despite the desperation behind her CB activities) is predominantly a perceptive and level-headed person. Realizing that Pam knows him better than either of his boys, Floyd gives forth with his most sustained, revelatory, and—in the way that it inadvertently prefigures his walk through the woods and involvement with Harold's cattle—prophetic speech.

> You see how I live? In a junkyard. I know that. Worked all my life—trucker. Now they call me Papa Thermodyne and I live in a junkyard. This country promises everything—sure. You never see. You ever see any of it, huh? I should'a stayed in Canada. Big deal. Missus wanted 'em raised Americans. Could'a had a cattle ranch there. Wasn't for him [Blaine] I could'a had cattle. I could'a been someone. See what I got? A lotta rusty doo doos. You look smart. If you're smart, you'll go to Canada. Gotta go through the woods. I'd go. I gotta stay for him.

Pam knows the self-deception in Floyd's speech, though, and calls him to account for it. After Floyd says, "I gotta stay for him," Pam says, "Well, I always thought it was the other way around." The whole family situation is based on a plethora of misconceptions and misstatements, with sons and father alienated from and misunderstanding each other.

Although *Citizens Band* eventually moves toward a series of resolutions, not all of them turn out that well. The reconciliation among Harold, Connie, and Joyce—with the three of them hesitantly deciding to live together—is meant to seem comic, but it is actually morally objectionable, a reunion taken too far. Harold may assert when all three sit down at a table in Debbie's mobile home that "Basically, I think we got a communications problem," but the truth is that it's precisely through Harold's perverse way of relating to people that the threesome have a problem to begin with. Moreover, Harold doesn't say they have a "communication" problem but one involving "communications," implying that it isn't the message about his deception of Connie and Joyce that is to blame but the medium that he used (the telephone) in juggling their relationships, another example of his refusal to accept responsibility for his actions. Moreover, the women's decision to share Harold seems less like a solution than an example of their diminished integrity, since they are still being exploited by him. (The meeting is hosted by Debbie, which makes Harold's duplicity that much more of an issue here.)

Although Blaine later finds out that Blood, who has been threatening him over the radio, is really his brother, Blaine is no closer to a satisfactory resolution of his problems, either. People are still hiding, either behind phony resolutions (as with Harold and his wives) or CB monikers. "Everybody in this town is somebody they're not supposed

Connie, Debbie, and Joyce converge for the meeting with Harold

to be," Blaine says. Pam thinks he's talking about Dean/Blood, but he's also including Pam's Electra persona, which he has discovered. Yet even when their masks are off, Blaine and Pam can't communicate. Pam tells Blaine, "Well, you're impossible to talk to." Yet Blaine does leave their meeting more resolute, going back to his father's one-man birthday party (which he had callously left to go see Pam) and telling Floyd, "I love you." It's a new expression for him, one which he must look away from Floyd in order to verbalize, but he says it.

Floyd is, after all, the CB father in the town. His nickname, "Thermodyne," suggests the conversion of heat (his passion for Canada) into motive power (in this case his leaving through the woods, most probably to go back to Canada). Given the failure of other means to personalize Union and bring its people together, what the town at this point needs is an outward disaster that will unite them. With the help of CBs, Union's citizens band together to locate Floyd (virtually all of the film's characters drive into the woods and, under Dean's direction, fan out to look for Floyd; even the Aryan, although he grumbles about everyone, is involved in the search). Watching the just-discovered Floyd riding one of Harold's lost cattle (which were set loose by Connie and Joyce as revenge for Harold's duplicity), Pam, standing next to Blaine, repeats her speech from the film's beginning (significantly minus the negative phrase "come on"), but does so this time directly

Pam and Blaine's wedding

into Blaine's ear. "There are a lot of voices out there but yours is different; I like it," she says. Only this time, what she's talking about is a voice actually attached to a recognizable person with whom she is involved, and whose complementary actions in both declaring his independence from his father and directly demonstrating his concern for him (via the search) finally show Blaine behaving in the mature way that Pam has all along wanted. And though Blaine at first doesn't look at Pam, indicating another possible failed communication (in this sense, Blaine is just like Dean, who had averted his eyes when Blaine confronted him about being Blood), Blaine does turn toward Pam at her statement's end. With what are ultimately shown as the good intentions behind Blaine, Dean, and Pam's actions, this particular love triangle is happily resolved.

Although everyone attending it is separated in cars, Blaine and Pam's marriage demonstrates electronics' proper use: to bring people together. After the ceremony (which is performed on the CB), Demme shows us that these people are no longer alone. As all of the characters drive off in their vehicles, Demme completes the film's elliptical action by bringing back the plot's formerly figurative intersecting circles of lives, making them into a concrete expression of moral progress: all of the departing characters physically cross each other's paths. Demme ends the film with a view of one of the characters' radio-controlled toy planes trailing a message of marriage congratulations: "Happy wedding Electra and Spider." This time, though, the CB handles have a positive connotation, because we know that the people behind them are in an honest, direct human relationship. By virtue of his film's humor and accepting tone, Demme has done more than bring unity to Union; he's also brought a feeling of warmth and purpose to the audience as well. Through the electronics of filmmaking, he's turned *Citizens Band*'s viewers into a global village of communally shared pleasure and goodwill.

4 | Problems on the Set

When a director with a distinctive style subjugates that style to another director's—as Demme does in his 1979 Hitchcock homage, *Last Embrace*—the results can be disappointing. This is not to say that *Last Embrace* might not have been a failure on its own terms. A film about a guilt-driven undercover agent trying to solve a series of murders that he thinks are committed by a secret society, it's a weak thriller, with very little to say about its ostensible themes: the relationship between passion and death, the contrasts and similarities between holy and profane love, and the various uses to which the past may be put. However, at best these ideas are merely grafted onto the film, never seeming to arise out of it. The result is the least successful film that Demme has ever directed, a judgment with which the director himself concurs.[1]

There is no way to speculate what *Last Embrace* might have been like if the script had been ready before shooting began and if the film's star, Roy Scheider, had been more cooperative during production.[2] Nonetheless, a great deal of what is wrong with the film may be ascribed to the efforts of its director. *Last Embrace*'s entire atmosphere—from Miklos Rosza's overly lush music (derivative of Bernard Herrmann's work) to Tak Fujimoto's usually effective moving camera, which is here subjugated to the most pedestrian of ideas, right down to the numerous (and unsuccessful) Hitchcock borrowings that dominate the film—tends to so strongly detract from what is supposed to be a taut psychological thriller that the end result is more tedium than tension. As Demme recalls: "I was kind of wallowing in style. I went into that movie thinking, Okay, here's a Hitchcockian thriller, and a lot of energy went into style more than into content."[3]

Other directors who admire Hitchcock have made their own homages to *Vertigo*, sometimes even devoting a complete film to the theme of the relationship among sex, death, and power, as Brian De

Palma did in *Obsession*. The problem with De Palma's film wasn't so much the imitation of the Hitchcock style (something Demme successfully manages in *The Silence of the Lambs*) as it was the actors: Cliff Robertson and Genevieve Bujold just couldn't bring as much intelligence and passion to their roles as Jimmy Stewart and Kim Novak did to Hitchcock's film. The absence of these characteristics is reflected in *Last Embrace*. Roy Scheider has none of Stewart's sophistication and wit, let alone his command of humor. Janet Margolin is hardly the locus of passion that Novak was in Hitchcock's work. But there are other problems with *Last Embrace*. The nervous breakdowns of Scheider's Harry Hannan don't seem very convincing. All it takes is for Jimmy Stewart to quiver and look faint in order for us to sympathize with the acrophobia that he is experiencing. Harry's fits—a spastic reaction in a paleontology lab and a sweaty, screaming awakening from a nightmare—seem like clichéd examples of what it means to be disturbed. And with Margolin's Ellie lingering in both scenes, sycophantically playing up to Harry, any sympathy we might have for Harry is very quickly dissipated by her irritating presence.

Even when Demme gives Harry his one big speech, during which he talks about how his wife was murdered and that it was his fault, we aren't very moved by what he is telling us. The emotions ring false because of Scheider's leaden acting. In the absence of any necessary identification with Harry, it is difficult to feel more than distance.

Like *Vertigo*, *Last Embrace* begins abruptly, in the middle of an action that becomes the cause of the protagonist's psychological dilemma. The scene in the restaurant with Harry and his wife, during which she is killed, is only a pale reflection of the rooftop chase in the Hitchcock film. The scene in Demme's film is meant to explain Harry's guilt about his wife dying during an ambush intended for him and provide an explanation for the anxiety that Harry is always feeling. Harry's involvement with Ellie, whom he first views as an innocent, is supposed to somehow deliver him from his problems. But the film never manages to work out this interaction in a satisfying way, merely showing us Ellie's two sides, sometimes as the innocent, sometimes as the homicidal avenger.

Last Embrace succeeds neither on the psychological level as a thriller about the attractions that the dead exert over us nor on a literal level as a drama, within which we might at least feel anxiety with regard to precisely who the Goel Hadam are and why they are after Harry. The film's subtext about the Jews is never developed; possible cross-references to the Holocaust and its implications for sexual abuse (as in the Nazis' use of Jewish women as prostitutes) are overlooked.

Ellie and Harry toward the end of *Last Embrace*

Where in Hitchcock the Goel Hadam linkage would merely be the Maguffin that propels the film along, in *Last Embrace* the idea is made to bear the impossible burden of unraveling the unbelievable actions that have gone on in the film. Demme apparently didn't realize that, at best, the Goel Hadam is a half-conceived notion, not the kind of idea that at the film's end would form the basis for a rewarding, O. Henry-like twist.

Neither the symbol-laden dialogue (for example, the references to hookers and prostitutes as "live ones") nor the overdone color symbolism (Ellie appears at a university reception wearing her grandmother's bloodstone jewelry) can redeem this film from mediocrity. In *Last Embrace*, Demme subsumes his stylistics to the most embarrassingly elemental of concepts.

As with *Last Embrace*, the script of *Swing Shift* (1983) was not complete when shooting began, yet ultimately this film caused Demme far more grief, and of a much different kind, than did the earlier film. Accustomed to formulaic star vehicle pictures, actress Goldie Hawn was reputedly very dissatisfied with Demme's treatment of the film; rather than speaking to Demme about it, she went directly to executives at Warner Bros. and told them that if *Swing Shift* were released in its present form, she would not honor her commitment to do any more films for the studio.

Hawn thought that her character was not portrayed as sympathetically as she should have been. Additional writers (Robert Towne among them) were brought in by the studio to rewrite certain scenes and to add others. Demme apparently refused to direct this new material, seeing it as a serious weakening of the film's meaning; however, because of a contractual obligation, he stayed on the set, watching as a team made up of Hawn and her associate, Anthea Sylbert, supervised shooting. This must have been a painful experience for Demme, to see a nearly completed work, on which he'd labored so much, eviscerated. *Swing Shift* had been expected to be Demme's "breakthrough" film; although critically appreciated for his earlier work, the director still had attained only slight public recognition.

Demme no longer discusses *Swing Shift*, yet his few previous comments reveal that his deepest regret is not for his own loss, but over the disagreements that occurred during the film's production. Soon after the film's release, Demme commented: "It was emotionally and psychologically very exhausting—but that wasn't about the horror of what can happen to you in the movie business, or the horror of a director having his movie taken away from him, though that was horrible. It was about being in sustained conflict with essentially decent people. Nobody giving in. It didn't sour me on anything except conflict."[4]

After the two screenings of the original Demme cut that were Demme's right under Director's Guild of America guidelines, Demme's version of *Swing Shift* was quietly shelved by the studio and replaced for theatrical distribution with Hawn's reworked version, which quickly bombed. It is legally impossible to see the director's intended version (although bootleg copies exist). Thus, it is necessary to summarize both the plot of the original *Swing Shift* and explain the focus that Demme intended the film to have in order to convey what a beautiful film *Swing Shift* originally was. The first script of *Swing Shift*, which was by Nancy Dowd (*Coming Home*), was later described by Demme as "an exposé of what was done to women working in the defense industries during World War II."[5] Bo Goldman then wrote the version that Demme first read, which was less political; when Demme became involved, he brought in Ron Nyswaner to further rework the material—all of this before the final rewriting under Hawn. The film's released version gives screenwriting credit to the fictitious Robert Morton.

More closely than the released version, Demme's *Swing Shift* probes the ways that American women at the time of World War II were limited by their prescribed roles and dramatizes the manner in which new opportunities for self-direction opened up for them as they entered the work force. Model wife Kay Walsh (Hawn) and "bad girl" Hazel Zanussi (Christine Lahti) become friends and coworkers in the MacBride airplane plant; ultimately, they shed and overcome the cultural stereotypes that previously limited them. Specifically, they break out of the dichotomy of fair maiden/dark temptress roles that Western culture imposes on women (*Last Embrace*'s Ellie and *Something Wild*'s Lulu/Audrey also exhibit these qualities).

Kay's husband Jack (Ed Harris) is much more overprotective of Kay in the original *Swing Shift*, much more just a nice guy who needs his consciousness raised. Jack's unwarranted hostility toward neighbor Hazel (at whom he yells "Tramp!" when he sees her pass by dressed for her job as sometime taxi-dancer, sometime singer) is more pronounced in Demme's version, as, conversely, is his insistence on sheltering his childlike wife, whose capabilities he constantly (if without malice) belittles. Jack's character most clearly articulates the social vision that "virtuous" women are to be cherished and protected, while "fallen" women must be vilified; unfortunately, the real women who are forced to fit into this model are allowed no middle ground between these dichotomies.

Ironically, the evening after the attack on Pearl Harbor, Jack and Kay listen to a radio broadcast by Eleanor Roosevelt, who was perhaps the prototype of the modern strong woman; an unforeseen result of the war about which Roosevelt is talking will be to offer women a liberation similar to Mrs. Roosevelt's own. When Kay, perched atop a stepladder, stretches to put black curtains over her home's windows in case of Japanese bombing raids, Jack not very helpfully lets her know, "You may be wasting your time." Kay replies, "I just want to give it a try." As she will show later, Kay is not afraid to take small steps in hopes of personal growth and larger rewards. However, as yet Kay has little faith in herself. When Jack ships out, Kay mourns, "I don't know what I'm going to do without you," to which Jack rather immodestly replies, "Me neither."

The ordering of key scenes was altered in the studio version, significantly changing their meaning; for example, the start of Lucky Lockhart (Kurt Russell) and Kay's relationship is different. In Hawn's cut, Kay reluctantly gives in to Lucky's repeated requests for a date (in Demme's version, Lucky has been asking Kay out for only three months, compared to five months in Hawn's) and goes with him to Kelly's bar *before* the Swing Shift Jamboree, after which they sleep to-

Kay, Lucky, and Hazel in *Swing Shift*

gether for the first time. Thus, when Hawn's Kay tearfully pleads with Lucky at Kelly's to leave her alone, she is still a faithful wife defending her chastity, instead of a guilt-stricken adulteress. Hawn seems to want her character to be as blameless as possible for the affair with Lucky, to seem more of a victim of fate than an independent woman making choices.

Demme's Kay is much more complex and adult than Hawn's. Lucky has stopped pursuing Kay by the time of the Jamboree; it is Kay who initiates contact with him that night by approaching him on the dock and impulsively asking for a ride home. Although Kay is afraid of what she is daring, the couple's decision to sleep together is mutual and mature (in Demme's version, Lucky caresses a nervous Kay's breasts; in Hawn's, Lucky charms Kay by cooking her an omelette). Demme's Kay acts to fulfill her own needs instead of unthinkingly subordinating herself in all things to Jack (as Lucky tells her, "You have the right to be happy"); Kay starts to take control of her life. Although she must still learn to balance her desires with those of others, Kay has started on the road to maturity.

In Hawn's version, Lucky *had* to come into Kay's house because of a rain storm, which led to his changing from his wet clothes into Kay's bathrobe (disrobing is frequently presented as titillating in mov-

Kay and Lucky's love scene in Demme's version

ies, since people supposedly "just can't help themselves" when less than fully clothed), and eventually to his presence in her bed.

In Hawn's version, the affair between Lucky and Kay goes on uneventfully and seemingly without much conflict until Jack's return. Demme's film showed a much more complex relationship between Lucky and Kay than Hawn's; Kay temporarily stops seeing Lucky *after* they first sleep together, not before, as in Hawn's version. Tensely trying to tell Lucky during their date at Kelly's that she has decided not to see him again, Kay spots one of her neighbors and, her fear of public opinion inflamed, panics and runs outside, to hide in the alley. Kay then begs Lucky to leave her alone. This Kay vacillates, at once daring to take the emotional support she needs from Lucky, and then fearfully backing down so as not to offend social mores. Consequently, although the scene is exactly the same in the two versions, when Demme's Kay cries in the alley outside Kelly's, her confusion is more complex, more real to us.

In both Demme's and the studio's versions, the camera closes in on Kay's face while MacBride worker Jeannie Sherman is crying after being told of her soldier husband's death; Kay obviously could be in this position herself at any time. Hawn's cut places this scene after the beginning of Kay and Lucky's affair, unconnected to its progress in any way. In contrast, Demme's cut followed this scene with the one in which Kay temporarily broke up with Lucky, thereby partially explaining her motivation for doing so. Demme then included a brief shot of the small, mournful funeral for Jeannie's husband, attended by Kay, who is standing bleakly among the other MacBride women to one side of the grave, with Lucky standing alone on the other. After the funeral, Lucky appears at Kay's door, and the two sadly and wordlessly embrace. In love with two men, Kay cannot bear to lose them both, although she is deeply aware of the ambiguity of her choice.

Many of Demme's usual concerns are present in *Swing Shift*. The opening sequence involves a street scene in which we see the whole of Kay and Jack's neighborhood throbbing with life. The camera pans along the sidewalk, moving from Jack walking home from work, to a kid on a bike, past Hazel watering her plants, to Kay, who, although she is dutifully waiting for Jack, already unconsciously bebops to Hazel's loud swing music. Throughout the film, swing symbolizes the liberating forces released by World War II that affected women and people of color and which would forever change the country's social patterns; in *Swing Shift*, swing is just beginning to affect mainstream Americans.

Demme's version is much more a telling of parallel stories of the two female leads. Scenes between Kay and Hazel are about equally weighted, making it more apparent that both women are undergoing a simultaneous liberation from social expectations—Kay from being a dependent wife, almost virginal in her innocence, and Hazel from being a "loose" woman not considered worthy of respect—and movement toward being what they choose to be. (Exemplifying the popular stereotype, their hair colors—Kay's blonde and Hazel's brown—reflect the women's supposed light/dark orientations.)

In Demme's cut, Hazel is not as fawning toward her boyfriend Bisquits (Fred Ward), who in turn is more obviously controlling and abusive of her. Like Jack, Bisquits treats Hazel as if she were a worthless floozy. Angry because Hazel stands up to his callous refusal to let her continue as a singer at his nightclub, the Egyptian Ballroom, Bisquits yells "Listen, you act like you don't make your livin' at the dance hall," as though the fact of her working there lowered her intrinsic value. When Hazel breaks off with him, it is to preserve her self-respect; their eventual reunion is possible only because Bisquits finally acknowledges Hazel's equality and acts to make amends.

Nor is it just these two women who learn to define themselves; by extension, all of the women who get jobs at the MacBride plant do so: African American women are among the new MacBride workers (black women were present in war industry factories in great numbers, leading to the urbanization of many African American families, yet in most movies dealing with women in the war industry they are totally absent). Also included is a woman with dwarfism, who tells Hazel that her previous best-paying job was as a munchkin in *The Wizard of Oz* (Hawn chose to dub in a more innocuous remark). While this line is humorous, it is also a genuinely sad comment on society's imposition of limitations on those whom it views as different.

This imposition of roles is seen throughout Demme's film via Kay's exposure to newsreels and the pep-rally speeches at MacBride,[6] during which she is told what actions are acceptable for her (those that coincide with the government's needs) and what actions are not. First, Kay is encouraged to help the country by working in the national defense industry, and is then told that she needs to work harder. Finally, at the end of the war, she is advised that it is in everyone's best interests for her to return home. Photographers seem to almost constantly lurk in the corners of the MacBride plant in order to gather material for more newsreels and articles to fashion opinions. Yet just as we see the physical mechanics of this image-making at work, so also do we see the reality behind the fictions that will be imposed. It is obviously not to Kay and Hazel and the other women's benefit to give up their well-paying jobs and go home. Demme's Kay moves away from her early unquestioned belief in this wartime propaganda, eventually going so far as to duck out of a MacBride inspirational speech in order to meet Lucky in a back room.

Kay needs to recognize the limiting modes of behavior that society has encouraged her to adopt. During her date with Lucky at Kelly's bar, Kay is upset by a photographer who tries to take her picture (she hides her face); she still worries about being labeled as unfaithful, about offending public opinion. In the midst of the couple's clandestine meeting during the MacBride speech (which only appears in the Demme version), Lucky tells Kay how stressful he finds the secrecy she has imposed on their relationship. In turn, Kay shows Lucky a nasty note that she found in her toolbox. "People know," she says. "They think I'm a tramp." She still sees only two dichotomous roles open for her and, at least in public, opts for the socially acceptable one.

Both Hazel and Lucky are initially associated with swing: Hazel sings, Lucky plays the trumpet. They're both more self-directed than Kay, who in scenes with Jack is frequently posed next to her pet canary as if she too were a captive songbird. Jack disapproves of swing, and Kay can only respond to its rhythm when her husband is present by being playful, a childlike, therefore supposedly less valid, response. Things start changing for Kay after Jack leaves and she begins work on the four o'clock to midnight swing shift; as Kay says to Lucky, "It's all so turned around." Economically and personally, Kay's life is changing rapidly because of the war. Even Lucky, when he teasingly explains away his requests for dates with her by saying to Kay, "Just trying to improve your taste in music," is attempting to help Kay find herself in this new world.

In Demme's version, Kay's questioning of her patriotic acceptance of the rationale that the newsreels have provided for the war begins with her exposure to Lucky's attitudes. The scene in which Kay approaches Lucky after the Jamboree was excised from the studio version in part because Kay was too bold in it, but also because Lucky seemed too much of a rogue. Lucky appears happy enough to be 4F and therefore exempt from the draft; he also seems quite cheerful when he tells Kay "I got a bad heart," a statement that has emotional meaning here as well, since Lucky has made it no secret that he is something of a predator with women. (Hawn's cut substitutes Lucky, in bed with Kay later that night, regretfully, even slightly guiltily, explaining his 4F status.) Like Kay, Demme's Lucky is mixed morally and emotionally—not an innocent as Hawn would have him.

In Demme's cut of *Swing Shift*, as in his other films, the director uses point-of-view shots to foster audience identification with characters. When Hazel and Kay are dressing for the Jamboree, we get Hazel's point of view of Kay in her prudish dress (of which Jack obviously approves); like Hazel, we think she looks silly with a high lace collar and long lace sleeves, but Hazel's reluctance to say so bluntly and hurt her friend evokes a more sympathetic response on our part as well. (Hazel's encouragement of Kay to act sometimes for herself is nicely depicted; when Kay explains that "Jack doesn't like revealing things," Hazel laconically replies: "Let him wear it.") Similarly, when Jack tells Kay (the audience literally seeing from her perspective) that he has joined the navy, we readily imagine all of the pain that this decision must cause her.

Demme is often subtly playful in his editing, rarely letting darker moods predominate. In *Married to the Mob*, Demme uses a badge-shaped iris to lead into the scene of Angela's absurd interrogation by the FBI. Here, the transition from Kay and Lucky's bleak reunion after the funeral to happier times includes a star-shaped iris, ultra-patriotism to the point of ridiculousness, reminding us of how these people are being manipulated by the government to support the war.

Just as Lucky is Kay's leadman at the MacBride plant, so too does he lead her in her quest for maturity. Inevitably, however, Kay must grow beyond her initial need for help; when Kay is also made a leadman after saving a coworker's life, it is apparent that she has grown sufficiently to function independently in the adult world that the MacBride plant represents.

The extent of Kay's metamorphosis into maturity is tested when Jack returns unexpectedly on leave. In Hawn's version, Kay is again a pawn of fate, reactive instead of active. Jack improbably guesses that she has a boyfriend, and she meekly promises to end her relationship with Lucky. Hawn includes a scene of Kay reading Jack's cliché-ridden and melodramatic goodbye letter, whose triteness only tends to trivialize their situation.

In contrast, Demme's Kay is active, not passive. First, Kay guiltily hides evidence of Lucky's presence in her untidy bedroom; Kay's messiness indicates how far Kay has swung away from her compulsively neat life with Jack. (Hawn titillates the audience by having Jack walk into Kay's tidy room and look in the closet, only to discover Kay's leadman shirt.) In a key scene removed from the studio version, Kay and Jack stroll on the beach, Jack trying to reconnect with Kay by planning their future, in which he expects they will essentially return to their past. "Everything's going to be great when I get back," he says, but Kay no longer feels the same and can't respond. Bewildered and therefore hostile, Jack again starts calling Hazel a tramp as he blames his wife's friend for Kay's newfound independence. At the beginning of the film, Kay had passively accepted Jack's abuse of Hazel; now, Kay defends Hazel against his unreasoned prejudice. When Jack wonders what has happened to his previously compliant wife, Kay retorts, "Only idiots smile all the time." Jack can't believe that Kay is capable of developing these strong opinions on her own. "Somebody's been puttin' some funny ideas in your head," he says. When Jack finally turns away, angrily saying "I can't even talk to you anymore," Kay realizes how far apart they've grown, and that the only thing that can possibly bring them together is forthright communication.

Demme's Kay chooses to confess her affair with Lucky to Jack. She wants to be honest with him, to act now with integrity; for someone as morally weak as Kay was initially, this is a wonderfully brave moment for her. Still reacting immaturely, Jack continues to blame Hazel for his problems; when later that day Hazel walks past him on her way home, Jack, brooding alone on his porch, glares at her the whole time.

Likewise, Hazel wants to confess to Kay immediately after Hazel and Lucky, both lonely and distraught, sleep together that night. "I don't think I can look her in the eye until I do," Hazel tells Lucky, who feels more aggrieved ("I'm the one with the broken heart, remember?" Lucky says). Kay is immediately put in the exact position in which she has placed her husband, that of the betrayed. Can she react maturely and with understanding? Although Kay values Hazel's friendship, she fails to really forgive her. The three attempt to reconcile at Kelly's bar, but Kay starts an argument in which, reverting to Jack's attitudes, Kay calls Hazel a "whore." Kay denies the emotional complexity of Hazel and Lucky's situation, refusing to accept that their despair and need for comfort were similar to her own, and tries to dismiss Hazel by labeling her a temptress; by doing so, Kay avoids addressing her own underlying problems.

Since Hawn's version stresses the film's love story aspects, her Lucky receives more emphasis than does Demme's. Demme's Lucky, who has only stayed at MacBride to be near Kay, quietly leaves for good after bringing a drunken Kay back home safely from the fiasco at Kelly's; he recognizes how compromised their friendship would be if he stayed and, presumably, does not want to again risk coming between her and Jack. As he leaves, Lucky pauses to look at himself and Kay in the mirror above her dresser; as in many Demme films (e.g., *Married to the Mob*, in which Angela stares at her reflection), such self-contemplation offers a bitter moment of self-knowledge.

Hawn's added dialogue and scenes continue to stress Lucky's centrality, however. Before he goes, Hawn's Lucky pleads, "Come with me, Kay," a request that she virtuously resists. Thus, Hawn's Lucky ignores Kay's immaturity, and is himself somewhat immature to want to continue with Kay despite knowing of her continued love for her husband. Hawn also has one final melancholy scene of Lucky on his band's tour bus, somewhere out East, reading a letter from Kay; Lucky seems unable to let go emotionally. This emphasis reduces the film to a domestic tragedy.

In both versions, Kay's rift with Hazel persists through the war's end and the women's layoff from MacBride. When Jack's ship docks, Kay meets him, and he seems more willing than before to accept her as an equal, thanking her for her offer to help him with his bags. However, Demme's Jack also sees the parallel between Kay's layoff and his own—an unconscious criticism of government policies that manipulate citizens' lives. (Hawn's version has Jack mumble a dismissive "That's tough," when Kay tells him that she has lost her job; Demme's Jack accepts the parallelism between their situations, saying, "Me, too.")[7] In Demme's version, Jack has truly adapted to Kay's financial and personal independence; no longer forcing women into the role of either saint or whore, he accepts the validity of Kay's feelings for someone else. Jack's change in attitude is confirmed when he approaches Hazel in a genuine spirit of reconciliation.

At a final party during which all of the MacBride women and their spouses get together, the women, grouped in the kitchen (to which they have been symbolically returned), mourn the respect and independence they have lost along with their jobs. Kay realizes at last that she cannot afford to lose Hazel's friendship too. (The two versions of the scene are the same, except for the inclusion in the studio version of a grouping of both the men and women in the living room before the dancing starts, suggesting more of a final social reunion of the sexes than Demme wanted to depict.) Significantly, Kay and Hazel forgive each other *outside* the house, demonstrating their escape, through reciprocal support, from the old idea of women's space.

This is also the final scene that Hawn chose to change. The revised version has a mutual reconciliation between Kay and Hazel, as though both had been equally at fault for their rift. Hawn removes the somewhat accusing lines that Demme's Hazel, whose back is to the camera, speaks. Demme's Hazel says to Kay (who has asked her to come outside), "You wanted something?" (By contrast, Hawn's Hazel remains silent). For Demme, Kay must acknowledge the wrong that she has done Hazel in denying her respect through assigning her a negative, stereotypical role; Kay must prove her maturity by accepting this responsibility. Thus, Demme's reunion of the two women not only demonstrates female solidarity and the importance of friendship, but also celebrates maturity and self-definition.

Demme's film has one final shot after Kay and Hazel hug. The two women are sitting alone on a beach at sunset, in silhouette, laughing and drinking beer and rhythmically kicking their heels in the air to an anachronistic, upbeat, synthesized melody on the soundtrack. The scene has a definite air of triumph. Unlike Hawn's characters, Demme's Kay and Hazel prefigure the modern feminist movement, which holds that women are able to make it on their own.

5 | Huck Meets the Hucksters

Melvin and Howard (1980) is a film about faith—in one's self, in the essential goodness of people, and in the ethic of free enterprise. This is not to say that the film is naive, that it endorses devotion to money and material goods for its own sake. Instead, what the film does is to examine this attitude and the strong attraction to it that many Americans have, doing so in the compassionate way that is characteristic of Demme's work.

Demme was offered *Melvin and Howard* after director Mike Nichols turned the project down. Initially, Demme was attracted because of Bo Goldman's script. As Demme remembers: "Whether he intended to or not, when Bo wrote *Melvin and Howard* he went on an amazingly poetic flight of imagination. To open a movie with an eighteen-page dialogue scene, two people riding along in a truck at night? Outrageous idea! It breaks every rule known to man, and yet the emotion he poured into that scene makes it wonderful."[1]

The subject matter, too, reflects concerns typical of the director; Demme sees Melvin as a prototypical common man. "It's a quintessentially American story. In the typical Hollywood version of that story, he would achieve his dream. But [the] screenplay remains true to the truth of the actual American Dream—that far more don't achieve it than do."[3]

As he had in *Citizens Band*, Demme used Paul Le Mat as his young proletarian hero, despite the studio's desire to cast Gary Busey as Melvin. Demme had also wanted Roberts Blossom (who played Le Mat's father in *Citizens Band*) as Howard Hughes, but the studio decided instead to cast a big name star, Jason Robards. *Melvin and Howard* won the 1980 best picture award from the National Society of Film Critics.[2]

With the exception of its opening and closing sequences, which involve Howard Hughes (or, at least, someone who claims that he is Hughes, although the old man's entrance into a Las Vegas hotel includes a view of a Rolls Royce at the frame's far right, suggesting that it is indeed Hughes), the majority of the film is either told from Melvin Dummar's point of view or is inundated with it. We're not, then, going to get an objective examination of America. Instead, what Demme sets out to do, and what he accomplishes, is to inquire into what it's like to be a true believer in America, to be someone who openly embraces the opportunities and oddities (and the concomitant problems associated with a devotion to capitalism) that characterize the nation. In this sense, Melvin is very similar to the greatest innocent ever to appear in American literature: Huckleberry Finn.

Like Twain's book, *Melvin and Howard* uses its main character as a foil against which it sets into relief all of the obsessions and foibles of America in order to effect social and political commentary. Although the technique goes back at least as far as Aesop's animal fables, the Huck Finn comparison is perhaps more appropriate because Melvin is so consummately American. Regrettably, he believes in money as a means to pleasure, in material goods as a sign of accomplishment. Here's a man who so strongly trusts in people's goodness that he's not even disappointed at the film's end when he knows that he's never going to get the sixteen million dollars that Hughes supposedly left him. What pleases Melvin most is that he and "Howard Hughes"[4] had a musical interlude together.

What Melvin is primarily concerned with is establishing a bond with the man whom he picks up in the desert, which he accomplishes through music. He doesn't care if the man claims he is Howard Hughes; how would Melvin verify it anyway? At the time that the film takes place, virtually no one had seen the reclusive Hughes for years. What counts isn't what the man's name is or how much money he has, but whether or not he'll sing along with Melvin's song. The song ("Santa's Souped-Up Sleigh") to which Melvin recites to "Hughes" the lyrics (which, like the present situation with his passenger in which Melvin finds himself, are concerned with a "mythical" character in whom you either do or do not believe) is more than just an example of Melvin's naiveté (he sent a company seventy dollars to have it set to music). It's clear that Melvin must have seen an ad for a tune-writing service at the back of a do-it-yourself magazine like *Popular Mechanics*, whose classifieds are filled with get-rich-quick or be-your-own-boss advertisements that would appeal to someone like Melvin. Melvin's reading these ads makes it plain that he wants to advance himself, but he doesn't know quite how. He's really nothing more than a rather uninventive laborer, a man who at first works in a magnesium plant, and later drives a milk truck.

"Hughes" and Melvin

For a few seconds after Melvin retrieves the old man, Melvin's pick-up truck passes through a rainshower. "There's nothing like the smell of the desert after the rain," "Hughes" says. A traditional film would use such a statement to suggest that there will soon be some fecund change in Melvin's life after this point. Yet the only thing that Melvin really wants is for the old man to sing along with him. Ridiculous as they are, the song's lyrics are emblematic of Melvin's character. "Santa's Souped-Up Sleigh" is about a time of happiness when, despite the season's materialistic associations, people are supposed to be responding to a true holiday spirit that involves the heart, not the pocketbook. Yet there's no unreal nostalgia for Christmas's good old days here; the song reflects a modern Christmas. Santa's sleigh is "souped-up," although the holiday doesn't suffer any compromise because of that; its essentially religious spirit of acceptance and love still remains intact. "Hughes" joins in with the song for a while and then, reluctantly, offers up a tune of his own, "Bye Bye Blackbird," a song in which the blackbird, an image of death, is banished by a woman who, orchestrating a touching rendezvous, "light[s] the light," setting it against the bird's darkness. "Bye Bye Blackbird" is thus as full of faith and hope as is Melvin. What Melvin and "Hughes" discover is that they're kindred spirits, materialists who also have a romantic side to them.

By contrast, when Melvin returns home to his trailer park abode, it's daylight, and everyone is asleep. When his wife Lynda (Mary Steenburgen) wakes up and sees that men are repossessing their motorcycle (another link with Hughes, who had been riding a motorcycle at the film's beginning), she decides to leave Melvin, taking their daughter Darcy (Elizabeth Chesire) with her.

Demme's approach to the more laughable aspects of American culture is always touching. Melvin and Lynda (who is at least seven months pregnant) eventually reunite and remarry in a Las Vegas professional marriage chapel.[5] The chapel is replete with canned music, tawdry decorations, and paid, resident witnesses. Demme spares us none of the details of the ceremony's preparations. Lynda is getting ready in one of the stalls of the chapel's bathroom; there's a woman in the stall to her right, who flushes the toilet and then leaves the room. Lynda emerges in a terrible blue dress (Melvin's outfit, replete with awful bow-tie, is just as bad) and begins to adjust her clothing in front of the bathroom mirror. Asking her daughter how she looks, she gets a comically truthful answer, "Fat . . . but nice." The chapel sequence combines qualities that are attractive (the Dummars' obvious devotion to each other) and repellent (the chapel's tawdry ambience), lending to the scene an atmosphere of nonjudgmental comic believability.

Melvin tells "Hughes," "I've had a lot of jobs but I can't seem to get the right one." Characteristically, he blames neither the jobs nor himself for his problems. Despite all of the disappointments Melvin experiences in the film, he never loses faith either in himself or the American way of life. In essence, he trusts in the power of self-confidence. Thus, when "Hughes" says that he is Howard Hughes, Melvin implies that this may very well be so, that one's faith takes precedence over the so-called facts of the material world. "I believe that anybody can call themselves whatever they want," Melvin says, thereby exemplifying Demme's view that true identity is more important than roles (this theme reappears in *Who Am I This Time?*, in which Harry Nash grows beyond his theatrical parts and into his real self). Names aren't important to Melvin; it's the person who counts. Here, the preeminence that Melvin assigns to faith tempers for us his strong belief in objects and advertising slogans and the huckstering associated with them (after the lessons of the film, though, Melvin spurns a quick-buck scheme about cashing in on the Hughes will by marketing tasteless T-shirts). Instead, it would appear that Melvin trusts in the truth of the soul as revealed through music, believing that no one could be lying about himself while singing, since the singer's approach to the song would reveal the real person. When "Hughes" protests that he has "an aversion to songs,'' thereby indicating that, at least for the time being, he has lost faith in the music inherent in the very fact of existence, Melvin tells him, ''that's what makes you an old asshole.'' He then gives ''Hughes'' an ultimatum: sing Melvin's song or walk. Compelled to accept Melvin's point of view, ''Hughes'' sings along.

Although both Melvin and Lynda regard television as a diversion, Melvin takes the medium far more seriously than does his wife: for him, it's a gateway into the world of materialism that he thinks, once realized, will solve all of his problems. Melvin thereby evidences a belief whose illusory status will be shattered when he ''inherits'' the money from Hughes, a situation that sets in motion objectionable forms of greed, violence, and exaggerated consumerism which Melvin up to that point had only tangentially experienced.

Melvin believes in the American Dream: lots of money and possessions. Even when he's working for the milk company as a driver, he wants to be milkman of the month, since the winner of the title gets a free television. Yet as Lynda points out to Melvin just before she leaves him for the second time, he can't tell the difference between the dream and harsh realities (although the ''reality'' in which Lynda believes is rather depressing). All that Melvin knows is that he wants to win on ''Easy Street,'' the game show at which, at least as a viewer, he excels (he always picks the right door, behind which is a wonderful prize). But Melvin is a dreamer/spectator only; when he actually participates in the show, or when he works at jobs, he fails (it's Lynda, the more practical-minded of the pair, who chooses the correct door when it really counts: when one of them is a contestant on the show ''Easy Street'').

Melvin's acceptance of other people's good luck is remarkable. When his daughter says of a prize winner on ''Easy Street,'' ''I'm jealous,'' Melvin responds to her with commercial slogans. The people who won are ''gonna fly the friendly skies; they're gonna lie in the sun.'' It's a consummation he wishes for himself as well. Melvin has what Lynda, referring to a book she has been reading, calls ''the magic of believing.'' Not only can Melvin pick the right doors when he watches the game show, he even has visions, as when, looking into a Las Vegas fortune wheel, he sees the face of the man who will deliver the Hughes will to him.

It's the desire for winning that propels Melvin and motivates him to get Lynda on ''Easy Street.'' Like the game show in Brian De Palma's *Sisters*, ''Easy Street'' is a wonderful parody of this peculiarly American construct. Hosted by Wally ''Mr. Love'' Williams, the show is a glamorization of greed, tinged, of course, with a little bit of sex. Just as the

Lynda and Wally "Mr. Love" Williams on "Easy Street"

men in the club where Lynda dances pay to gape at nude women, Wally juxtaposes sex and money, as when he says to Lynda (whose hands are cold) in a comically crude use of a sexual come-on, "You wanna put [your hands] in Uncle Wally's pocket?"

Melvin and Lynda's winnings bring out Lynda's extremely practical nature, one she has had to adopt when dealing with a dreamer like Melvin. When Melvin wants to buy an expensive, unaffordable house, Lynda objects. "I won the goddamn money and we'll take [the less costly house]," Lynda tells him. But Melvin can't resist being excited like a child at their winnings. When he comes home one day driving a red Cadillac that is towing a boat, Lynda once again decides to leave him. Melvin tries to explain why he wants the car, but his destructively acquisitive bent can't compete with her rationality, and we really can't blame her. As she points out, it's the first time they've been out of debt, and now Melvin has plunged them back into it.

Melvin and Lynda measure wealth in different ways. "We are poor, Melvin," Lynda says at an early point, to which Melvin replies, "We're not poor—broke maybe." Lynda's word "poor" refers to money; Melvin's refers to a spiritual poverty, a realm that, at least at this point in their lives, his level-headed wife can't afford to deal with if she is going to keep her family together. When Lynda once again tells Melvin that she's leaving, the conceptual split between the couple has never seemed greater.

Lynda: C'est la vie, Melvin.
Melvin: What's that?
Lynda: It's French. I used to dream I'd be a French interpreter.
Melvin: You don't speak French. [For once Melvin is referring to actualities.]
Lynda: I told you it was a dream.

Melvin can't see the relevance of this exchange. Most of the time, it's Melvin who is the dreamer and Lynda who rejects the dream for the harsh realities that she takes pride in accepting. Melvin views the dream as reality; Lynda feels impatient with her husband because he treats the dream as real, just as he does his own dreams. Melvin's dream of having a car like his new red Cadillac, a car similar to the ones that in his youth he'd seen going by so fast that you could hardly see them, is something that Lynda can't afford to share.

After marrying Bonnie (Pamela Reed)—whose business sense seems as still-born as Melvin's given the couple's poor luck with their gas station, and whose Mormon status ironically links up with the Mormon church's objection to the Hughes will—Melvin meets the stranger who comes into the station one day on the pretext of buying a pack of cigarettes and asking directions (still in love with one of consumerism's main bulwarks, advertising pitches, Melvin can't resist citing to the man the Camel slogan: "That's a man's cigarette; you'd probably walk a mile for these"). Yet when the Hughes will's existence is revealed, it unleashes the wild dogs of avarice and marketing mania in a lust for money with which Melvin can't cope. Like Yossarian in *Catch 22*, Melvin watches madness from the sheltering safety of a distant tree. The will isn't a wish come true but a nightmare. When a reporter asks Melvin if he ever dreamed that something like the inheritance would happen to him, he replies, "When you dream about something it's not a problem, but . . ." And hostility (present in the form of a man who drives up to the station one day and pulls a gun on Melvin) reigns even during the trial about the will's validity. When Melvin is called to testify, we can't tell which lawyer is his and which is the prosecutor; they're both equally nasty.

This overt madness reminds Melvin that what counts is not money (which by itself hasn't seemed to bring happiness to Hughes or anyone else for that matter) but what happens between people, some-

The crazed gunman in *Melvin and Howard*

thing that Melvin knew at the film's beginning. The truth comes back to Melvin at the film's conclusion when he realizes that he has no prospect of getting the inheritance, and when the highway is about to bypass his and Bonnie's gas station. Melvin says "it's all right" if he doesn't get the money because "Howard Hughes sang Melvin Dummar's song . . . he sang it, he was funny. Yeah, he sang it, 'Santa's Souped-Up Sleigh.'" (To Demme, this is the key line of the film.) At *Melvin and Howard*'s end, as the Demme ellipsis closes, with Melvin finally having realized that what's important isn't money but people (although it's still doubtful that Melvin is any more practical than before), the film's action returns to its beginning. We see "Hughes" alone (Melvin, who is asleep, is pragmatically not really present), not seen from Melvin's point of view, but there, really there. Unprompted this time, "Hughes" sings "Bye Bye Blackbird," sharing Melvin's vision in the liberating, loving power of music to bring people together, whether it be in song or through the music of a belief in humanity's goodness.

As a television news show in the film notes, Hughes dies at Easter. When the newscast goes on to remark on Hughes's own (Dummar-like) dream, the Spruce Goose, the plane that shouldn't fly but does, it's clear to us that the real Hughes's believing spirit, which knew his plane could fly, has, through "Hughes's" reappearance at *Melvin and*

Howard's end in the song sequence, been resurrected, reborn into life everlasting on the wings of the blackbird. At the film's conclusion, "Hughes" triumphantly rides the musical blackbird of death to life, love, and compassion (the suggestion here is that, if only for a second, "Hughes," like Melvin during their duet, has realized through a moment of special happiness that money will never bring either of them this kind of simple pleasure). Given the elation that this last scene causes in us, we might miss the significance of the end title that tells us that *Melvin and Howard* "was filmed . . . where the events actually occurred" (a sense of factuality complemented by Demme's having the real Melvin Dummar appear in a small role). In other words, the *film* believes that it was Hughes whom Melvin picked up, and that Melvin and Hughes for one brief moment shared a transcendent trust in the essential goodness of people that simply can't be measured in terms of dollars and sense.

6 | Imitation of Life

Who Am I This Time? is arguably Demme in his most pure form: all of his major themes—disguise and ultimate realization of identity, the redemptive power of love, the importance of community—are to the forefront, and are developed fully (years before his best films that expand on these concepts, *Something Wild* and *Married to the Mob*) in less than an hour. Demme directed this film, an adaptation of a Kurt Vonnegut, Jr., short story, in 1982; it was aired as part of the PBS American Playhouse series.

Under the credits, we get peaceful views of a small town that look forward to those shots in *The Silence of the Lambs* that show us Belvedere, Ohio, and the town in which Clarice Starling grew up. *Who Am I This Time*'s shots convey a sense of rural ease that suggests an uncomplicated approach to personality, one unaffected by the stresses of big cities and the neuroses that go along with living in them. This attitude is true for the majority of the people in the town of North Crawford, but not for the film's two principals, Helene (Susan Sarandon) and Harry (Christopher Walken), an aspect that makes it clear that for all of the small-town simplicity connoted by the opening shots, Demme doesn't intend to abandon his interest in complex characters.

The story of *Who Am I This Time?* gives Demme a chance to deal directly with his major theme of people's adopting roles that, while liberating, paradoxically hide their true selves; yet ultimately a synthesis is formed that allows communication and union. Interestingly, what is charming in Demme was originally slightly condescending in Vonnegut. This distinction is most apparent in each man's treatment of the character who functions as the author/director's surrogate, George Johnson (Robert Ridgely). Vonnegut's George remains distant and ironic, slightly pitying but definitely superior to the difficulties of Helene and Harry. Since George is also the narrator of the short story, his is the view we adopt in the end. In contrast, Demme's George is not ironic at all—he is almost a teddy bear of a man, nonjudgmental and genuinely helpful. His good humor is the grace note that sets the tone for the whole film, allowing the audience to feel nothing but pleasure when Harry and Helene finally get together. (As Northrop Frye notes regarding this trope in comedy that goes back to Shakespeare and the Greeks, the marriage of two lovers reunites and renews the entire community. Indeed, the film's delight in community is present from its very beginning, with the placid shots of people's homes and lawns.)

George becomes director of the North Crawford Mask and Wig Club when its longtime director, Doris (Dorothy Patterson), steps down; as Doris says, "It's time the company developed some new talent." Demme's note of Doris's face as she says this (she shows some pain but also a determination to be generous as she starts the cast's applause for their new director) reflects his own sensitivity to the importance of allowing a plurality of speech. In turn, George is eager as director to allow his actors to develop themselves.

Demme expands from Vonnegut on the question of the nature of identity by beginning his film with the group performing *Cyrano de Bergerac*, perhaps the most poignant play ever written dealing with the subject of identity. (The scene opens on Cyrano's "Who are you? . . . my ancient enemies," a speech in which he questions his own failings.) Cyrano's inability to reveal his love to Roxanne except through the physically attractive medium of Christian parallels Harry's inability to make contact with others except when he is releasing his inner passions through acting, and foreshadows the way in which he will ultimately make love to Helene.

George goes to the hardware store where Harry is clerk to ask him to audition as Stanley in *A Streetcar Named Desire*. Harry only deals with unemotional issues at the store, such as counting nuts and bolts; when he is forced to interact without an assumed persona, he can hardly function (similarly, Helene deals primarily with machines in her job with the phone company). We learn later that Harry's isolation stems from his having been a foundling—not only is he cut off from community, he doesn't even know his own family. When Harry accepts George's offer by saying "Who am I this time?" his words indicate his lack of identity.

George meets Helene by chance while contesting his bill with the telephone company. (Like the CB radios in *Citizens Band*, telephones act as a substitute for direct human communication.) Disputing a long-distance call to Hawaii for which he has been erroneously billed ("I don't think anyone in North Crawford has ever called Hawaii—or ever will for that matter," George says), George confronts Helene, who is in

charge of the new automatic billing machines that have caused
George's problem, and who spends only eight weeks in each town
starting up the system. Helene, who at this point seems more an extension of the machines with which she travels than anything else,
apologizes for the billing error in an emotionless monotone. After she
explains the functions of the new computer system to him, he jokingly
remarks, "As long as people come along with the machines we don't
have anything to worry about. It's when the machines start delivering
themselves that we have a problem." Helene doesn't respond, though;
at this point she barely qualifies as human.

Apparently struck by Helene's good looks (a reaction to her appearance only, not yet to her inner self), George invites her to audition
for *Streetcar*. "Have you ever acted?" he asks. Aside from its literal
meaning, the question suggests the possibility that Helene has never
taken charge in her life, being content to merely let things happen to
her. The invitation's dual meanings shock Helene into responding for
the first time in a human way; she looks George hesitantly in the eyes
and departs from her phone company "script." "I've been going from
town to town for two years and that's the very first time anyone has
ever approached me about participating in a community thing," she
says. Helene reacts to the idea of being a part of something, a member
of a group. George reinforces this idea: "There isn't any other way to
get to know a lot of nice people faster than being in a play."

It would seem that both Harry and Helene are waiting to be res-
cued, almost as though they have been waiting all their lives for the
other one to come along. When they audition together, they become
their characters so completely that they throw away their prompt
books and still continue to deliver the play's lines. For the sake of the
story we ignore an absurdity: that both characters know their parts so
quickly because they've been vicariously living them for so long. We
accept the fact that the words that Harry and Helene shout at each
other perfectly match those of Tennessee Williams's *Streetcar* because
we want to witness the union of art and life that these two characters
so desperately need. Only by enjoying themselves within the protected world of a fiction will they finally be able to gain the self-assur-
ance necessary to allow them to live comfortably in the "real" world.

Early during Helene's audition, she is unable to show any emotion,
real or feigned. Prodded by George to remember some personal experience that may help her, she explains that even as a child, she moved
so frequently that she never connected with others emotionally, except maybe with the stars of motion pictures. Helene still has great
difficulty in the present when meeting anyone: "I want to, but I feel

like I'm in some kind of glass bottle, as though I can't touch the person no matter how hard I try." George regretfully gives up.

As often happens in a Demme film, however, people initially acting under other identities eventually drop their masks and help each other through a process of redemption. Harry enters, in character as Stanley, for his audition; he addresses Helene as Stella and demands that they start playing their scene. The camera, shooting from Stanley/Harry's point of view, gives a frightened/intrigued/aroused Helene "the eye," panning from her head to her feet. In return, Helene "watches" Harry strip off his shirt to a heartbeat-like throbbing as the camera moves closer to Harry and then back.[1]

A few minutes before, Demme included another point-of-view shot as Helene watched Doris exhort her to show some emotion as Stella. In the scene that follows, as Harry and Helene give increasingly spirited readings, Demme throws in more point-of-view shots as the two are facing each other, encouraging us to identify with the feelings of these two outsiders. We don't feel superior to them as we did in the ironic Vonnegut original.

As rehearsals for *Streetcar* commence, it is apparent that Helene is becoming increasingly emotionally liberated by her acting as Stella and by her growing attraction to Harry. One night after the rehearsal, she lets George know that she has told the phone company that she wants to stay in North Crawford from now on. Aware of Helene's attempts to make real her newfound emotionality, George is afraid for her, and says somewhat evasively, "as a director I'm very happy." This is not enough for Helene, who wants a real (as opposed to theatrically oriented) response. "What about George Johnson?" she asks. George finally accepts her challenge to make their friendship more personal, and replies, "If I had a daughter, I'd like one just like you."

Helene also tries to get closer to Harry. In a bittersweet scene (not in the short story), Helene invites a reticent Harry to eat lunch with her during rehearsals. It turns out that she has brought a giant picnic basket full of food she's cooked for him, and she leads him to a corner of the stage that happens to be in front of a crudely painted backdrop of a countryside. When Helene spreads a red and white checked tablecloth and the couple sit on the floor before the backdrop, the camera slowly moves in until the rest of the stage is obscured. It's as if Harry and Helene are truly having a picnic lunch; once again, the division between what is real and what is affected blurs.

Unfortunately, Harry can't respond to Helene without artifice to help him; during their "picnic" he nervously avoids her look and mutters answers to her questions, until he flees when, unaware that he is a foundling, Helene asks him about his mother's cooking. Helene feels guilty about her unintended insensitivity; as Harry first helped her to find her feelings during the audition, Helene now wants Harry to change and be open.

Lydia, who has starred opposite Harry previously and is also his employer, tries to warn Helene of Harry's real inability to communicate. "Once a play is over, whatever you thought Harry was just evaporates into thin air," Lydia says. Helene refuses to listen.

However, immediately before the curtain goes up on *Streetcar*'s first performance, all of the cast members are hurriedly going over their lines in their playbooks one last time—except Harry, who at this point, on the verge of the play's enactment and apparently already in character, is the one person who is most at ease (he's standing across the stage, smiling at Helene).

Significantly, when the curtain rises to present the cast at the end of the first performance, Harry and Helene are caught unaware, still holding hands and gazing into each other's eyes, an indication that there is an outside reality to their relationship that threatens to escape the confines of the play. All the more reason for Helene to be stunned when, moments later, she turns to hand Harry one of her congratulatory roses and he has disappeared. In an attempt to help him directly, Helene goes to the hardware store, where Harry is besieged by teen-aged fans (whose confusion between art and life is comic: they call Harry "Stanley"). He falls back on his role as clerk ("Can I help you?"), much as Helene had in her first conversation with George. While Helene, looking aside, tries to explain the feelings of inadequacy that he has unintentionally helped her to overcome, Harry slips away. Helene is hurt, and at that night's performance she is unable to respond to Harry's acting. She can't use artifice any longer without the acknowledgment that there is an independent reality too.

Helene has found a solution to Harry's problem by the third and final performance, however. After the curtain calls, she refuses to let go of Harry's hand, forcing him to remain with her on stage to accept congratulations, then giving him as a present a leather-bound copy of *Romeo and Juliet*. Of course, she wants him to read aloud her favorite scene with her, Romeo and Juliet's meeting in the garden during which Juliet learns Romeo's true identity. "What's in a name?" Helene/Juliet asks Harry, and—as the Shakespeare play suggests—it is the endemic qualities of personality, not the superficial social ones, that are the most important. Harry and Helene can finally laugh happily together. Yet, paradoxically, they could only reach this point through artifice.

Helene and Harry outside of the department store

The film ends with a nice coda that again stresses the idea of the mutability and endurance of identity, with Harry asking Helene to marry him by acting out the proposal scene from *The Importance of Being Earnest*. Earnest, himself a foundling, has won Miss Fairfax's heart while acting under an assumed name, just as Harry has done with Helene. By this point the layers of meaning regarding Helene and Harry's identities seem hopelessly, but wonderfully, mixed. We as audience are watching truth within a play within a play.

The love scene is interrupted when Helene realizes that all of her and Harry's friends are standing around them watching, prompting the group's applause. In reply to George's request that Helene and Harry star in the club's next play, Harry whispers in Helene's ear, and she repeats his question: "Who are we this time?" Although the question is an echo of Harry's earlier reply to George, the meaning at this point has changed completely. The singular (as noted earlier, Harry's question had been, "Who am I this time?") is now plural, implying not just the union of Harry and Helene, but their reintroduction into the community of North Crawford.

7 | Many People Clapping, One Man Rapping

There's a striking similarity between the art of *Swimming to Cambodia*'s Spalding Gray and David Byrne. In *Stop Making Sense* (1984),[1] Byrne keeps himself fairly devoid of reactions during his performance, but he does shade his voice as Gray does, and he employs stunning physical gestures that dramatize what's going on in his songs, now jerking back and forth in time to the music; or stumbling along the stage during "Psycho Killer" in order to exemplify the movements of a homicidal maniac; now running around the set; or using the famous "arm chop" gesture during "Once in a Lifetime" as an adjunct to the song's concern with psychological displacement.

In both films, there's an interest in the theatrics that cause an audience to become engaged in the concertgoing experience. If there are no pronounced politics in *Stop Making Sense* (just the implication of some in the band's multiracial aspect), that's no fault of the film, since its sensibility—playful, irreverent, and built upon driving, insistent rhythms—is justification enough. What distinguishes Demme's work in *Stop Making Sense* is the director's self-effacement (a quality evident to a lesser degree in *Swimming to Cambodia* [1987]). Indeed, what Demme is giving us here borders on a new type of documentary, one not interested in promoting a particular point of view, one that doesn't discover its subject matter in the process of filmmaking. As near as possible, what we have in *Stop Making Sense* is an accurate recording of events, highlighted by a soundtrack that attempts to do justice to the sonics of a typical Talking Heads concert.

Stop Making Sense intends as much as possible to recreate the concertgoing experience for us (the footage is from three performances at the Hollywood Pantages Theatre in December 1983). The occasional rapid cutting and close-ups don't prevent us from becoming fully engaged in the film; in fact, these techniques act as corollaries for the way that a concertgoer might shift his or her eyes from one part of the stage to another or, through concentration, might seem to zero in on a certain musician.

The film begins with a close-up of a shaft of light playing across a stage, into which David Byrne—or, to be more precise, Byrne seen only at shoe level—moves.[2] As the camera pulls back a little ahead of Byrne and pans up to reveal him, we realize that this is going to be a carefully controlled and structured film, but one that doesn't make its structure very obvious. In contrast to the emotional and artistic excesses of Goldie Hawn's version of *Swing Shift* (from which Demme sought relief by working on the Talking Heads film), *Stop Making Sense* is a model of restraint. Although Demme stylizes the film through cutting and changes in camera angle, he counts on the film audience's involvement in the concert event to avoid seizing on these details. In both *Stop* and *Swimming*, the films' styles are meant to enhance the concert experience, not draw attention to themselves.

Stop Making Sense builds slowly. Byrne comes out with no accompanist, merely a boom box and his acoustic guitar. The song with which Byrne chooses to open the show ("Psycho Killer") is pared down, too—a simple song about an individual whose convoluted mentality is first inner-directed and then, at aberrant moments, results in explosions of violence (a behavior that looks forward to the psychology of Jame Gumb in *The Silence of the Lambs*). The song moves us from a small, insular world to a larger one full of expansive threats, conditions mirrored in our realization that the concert, at this point an intimate communication between Byrne and the film viewer, is nonetheless taking place before a large number of people. What Demme seems to find in the concert atmosphere, then, is an experience that is individual yet communal. And since *Stop Making Sense*'s communication is meant to be achieved in a theatre, the group experience—an integral part of concertgoing—is, ideally, recreated every time the film is exhibited as well. We watch the film as individuals but are always aware of other audience members' reactions around us. The movement from the individual event, through the group, and back to the individual makes the Demme ellipsis complete.

The film with which *Stop Making Sense* invites comparison is Martin Scorsese's *The Last Waltz*, which is dominated by the personality of The Band's Robbie Robertson, and which features Scorsese himself in the role of a documentarist asking Robertson and other group members (who only talk occasionally) questions. In *Last Waltz*, Robertson irritatingly occupies center stage all of the time. From the blocking of the scenes and the studio-shot waltz that ends the film, we sense in *The Last Waltz* that Scorsese may have stylized and structured

David Byrne in the Big Suit

his film a bit too rigidly. These qualities aren't in evidence in *Stop Making Sense*. Byrne may be in front of the camera and Demme behind it, but each makes himself unobtrusive enough to let the concert speak for itself.

One of the characteristics that distinguishes *Swimming to Cambodia*[3] from the rest of Demme's films is that it is a production about a single individual. While other films such as *Melvin and Howard* filter their action through a central consciousness, none concerns itself with one person as the focus of everything. Yet Spalding Gray isn't really alone up there on the stage: he's assisted by graphics, music by Laurie Anderson, and intercut scenes from director Roland Joffé's *The Killing Fields*. In a strict sense, though, even without this support, Gray isn't conceptually alone. Gray becomes "Gray" and other people as well, as when he takes on the voices of individuals such as Ivan, Renee, and Jim Bean, the man with his finger on the nuclear button, a dual role assumption by Gray that Demme complements by rapidly cutting together shots taken from the left and right sides of Gray's table (all of this orchestrated in time with Gray's head movements) in an analogue of the traditional Hollywood two-camera setup, so that we can fully enter into the spirit of the dramatization that Gray is creating.

The problem that a famous Zen meditation aide poses is, "What is the sound of one hand clapping?" A similar kind of meditationlike focusing effect occurs when we watch *Swimming to Cambodia*, which concentrates our attention on the sound of one man rapping. Make no

Spalding Gray on course

mistake about it, though: we should no more assume that it is the literal Spalding Gray up there talking than we should believe that it is Anthony Hopkins the actor (rather than Hopkins as Hannibal Lecter) who kills the two police officers in *The Silence of the Lambs*. Moreover, there's an important transference that the act of storytelling or being filmed causes, and that's what we see operating in *Swimming*. In essence, Gray creates the Spalding Gray persona in the process of relating his tales; what's more, he simultaneously objectifies himself as raconteur (he is a voice speaking about itself) and personalizes himself in the sense that he repeatedly has us identify with the mass of idiosyncratic details with which we are presented.

But with whom are we really identifying? In *Studies in Classic American Literature*, D. H. Lawrence recommended that when evaluating works of literature, we should trust the tale, not the teller.[4] Gray's method, though, inverts this behest. We may not trust the tales (some of them, despite Gray's statement that with one exception they're all true, seem a little too pat, a little too exaggerated), but by virtue of Gray's affably neurotic presence, we do tend to trust the teller, and this trust seems to carry over to the credence that we assign to most of the stories. At the helm of a strangely fashioned rhetorical ship, Gray takes us on a sea voyage of self-examination and self-indulgence, ultimately leaving us pleasantly adrift at the film's end.

Swimming to Cambodia is a film about the politicization of a typical American (which is, after all, what Gray sets himself up to be; for an hour and a half, he is our guide through the national consciousness). Curiously, it's a politicization that occurs as a result of a movie (surely if Gray can become politicized by becoming involved, not with the actual war in Cambodia but with *The Killing Fields*, can't we expect the same effect by our being exposed to Gray's exposure to the politics inherent in Roland Joffé's film?). Yet for the most part, the majority of the politics to which Gray is exposed is a fiction. That's not real war smoke in *The Killing Fields*; it's the smoke from burning tires. People in Joffé's film aren't covered with real blood but chicken entrails. It's all an illusion. If that's so, what can we expect from *Swimming to Cambodia*, itself a media event that places us at an even further distance from the war's realities?

What Gray intends to make plain to us through his everyman responses, stylized though they may be, is that we have a strangely bipolar reaction to war. In one sense, like the men in what Gray refers to as the "flying Holiday Inns," who drop their bombs by computer, we never get emotionally involved in contemporary wars. The stories we read or hear about a war's realities, about what happens to the troops on the ground, are filtered back to us through the media. The real war is at a safe remove. What we witness in *Swimming* is the paradoxical experience of a man exposed to a faked representation of a war telling us through a comparably unreal theatrical situation about real responses to real situations from which, by virtue of our being only an audience at Gray's show, we are protected but to which we are expected to react. Yet, ironically, it would seem that we need fictions in order to tell us the truth about ourselves. *The Killing Fields* attests to this response, as does *Swimming to Cambodia*.

The other conceptual half of *Swimming* is involved with the Gray character's search for what he refers to as a "perfect moment," which, curiously, he does not find by acting in a film in which he strongly believes (in any case, later in his monologue Gray parodies his faith in Joffé's film). We might be outraged by the disjunction between *Swimming*'s two conceptual halves, yet the film makes the two strands coalesce. Thus, Jim Bean, the man whom Gray meets on the train to Chicago, who works in a waterproof room where he's ready to push the button to blow up the Russians, is the analogue of those pilots in the B-52s who blithely drop bombs on the Cambodians, as well as the counterpart of Gray's New York City upstairs neighbor, who inconsiderately turns on her loud music late at night.

We might get impatient with Gray's enthusiasm regarding his search for a self-indulgent perfect moment were it not that he keeps implicitly reminding us (mostly by returning to stories about *The Kill-*

ing Fields) that there is a real connection between personal self-indulgence and self-indulgence on a national scale. What Gray is really investigating in *Swimming to Cambodia*, then, is the psychology of the United States.

Indeed, the whole focus of the film has less to do with Gray as a central consciousness leading us through the experience of a number of seemingly unconnected events than with one person's realization of political awareness. A glance at the monologue's published version[5] indicates that fully two-thirds of it was excised for *Swimming*, partially because it was too long for a film but primarily, we believe, because the deleted information didn't contribute to the creation of the idea on which Gray and Demme decided the film should concentrate: what it means in the late 1980s to be political.

Gray is the perfect foil for this kind of inquiry. He's white and middle class, attributes made clear when he talks at one point about how his neighbors in "white-bread homogeneous . . . brick-wall Boston" would respond to his requests to turn down their music because they all spoke "a common language," a function of their shared racial and socioeconomic upbringing. This situation changes when Gray moves to New York City, which, in military terms, is more like a battlefield compared to Boston's sedateness. The shift in locales makes more understandable Gray's characterization of Southeast Asia, where the kind of aggressive American tendencies he finds in his contentious New York City upstairs neighbors are directed against the Cambodians, whose philosophy of *sanug* (pleasure), and almost-too-polite acceptance of the injustices being perpetrated against them, make us seem barbaric by contrast. Thus, when the Americans come through a Cambodian town distributing money to people whom they've accidentally bombed—"$100 bills to people who had lost family . . . and fifties to people who had lost arms or legs"—or when Gray reads a letter to the American ambassador that Prince Sirik Matak writes, which is full of gentle protests and remarkable resignation to unpalatable facts, we as Americans should be ashamed of what we're hearing. Just as in Vietnam, we used the Cambodians for our own narrow political ends; we set them up and then, when it suited us, abandoned them.

The problem, though, is that as a country we don't seem to have a sense of national shame, an attribute that might prevent the reoccurrence of similar events in the future. When Gray repeats the refrain about Roland Joffé, "leave it to a Brit to tell you your own history," he's making the point that only when we attain a certain distance from what happens to us will we be able to gain a proper understanding of ourselves. Not even the diplomatic corps has any real sense of politics, as is made plain when Joffé, reacting to Gray's protest that maybe he shouldn't be in the film because he's not political (Gray says that he's "never even voted in [his] life,") says, "Perfect, we're looking for [someone to play] the American ambassador's aide."

The American ambassador himself, whom Gray and the man playing the ambassador meet, doesn't seem to have any realistic political awareness either. His talk about Cambodia as "a ship floundering in high seas" (Gray compares the man to a cross between a ship's captain and a boarding school principal) distances him from political reality through cliché. Unintentionally, though, Gray's film also has a similar distancing effect. We realize that Gray is trying to be entertaining at the same time as he is attempting to convey important political points, but (to appropriate the words of Alain Robbe-Grillet about the traditional novel) do we really need the entertainment "sauce" here to make the political "fish" go down easier?[6]

But then, perhaps this is an unjustified objection. Accepting *Swimming* as a composite work that has dimensions of both entertainment and politics is probably what we should do. Nevertheless, it's difficult to avoid contrasting the film with Demme's two documentaries, *Haiti: Dreams of Democracy* (1987) and *Cousin Bobby* (1991). These films entertain, yet they do so by honestly conveying the political realities with which they are concerned: life in post–Duvalier Haiti in the former film, existence in Harlem in the latter, situations that in themselves are certainly engaging enough.

We know from *Haiti* and *Cousin Bobby* that Demme is strongly concerned with revolutionary politics. *Haiti* makes it quite plain that for Demme, only a regime responsive to the people's needs deserves support, regardless of which country we're talking about. The same is true in *Cousin Bobby*, an angrier film than *Haiti*, which shows us how the residents of Harlem have to cope with degrading living conditions while their pleas for urban renewal are repeatedly rebuffed. In both films, discontent leads to revolt; the result is the buildup of a significant anti-government movement in Haiti and civil unrest in the United States (although the cautionary tone is much more powerful in *Cousin Bobby*, which ends with comment-free shots of the 1965 riots in Los Angeles and the 1967 uprisings in Boston, Newark, and Detroit).

What is most striking about *Haiti* and *Cousin Bobby* are those characteristics that link up with the general political trends throughout all of Demme's films and the connections that the films establish between music and political awareness, another prominent aspect of

Demme's work. Throughout *Haiti*, information about conditions on a national scale (for example, the suppression of individual rights by the Duvalier regime and all of its successors) alternates with comments on those conditions not only by individual citizens but also by musical performers, the content of whose work is decidedly political. At various points, Demme has taken songs by groups such as Foula and Fréres Parents (the latter of whose music appears briefly in *Married to the Mob*) and has, essentially, mounted music videos for them. The obvious comparison between these sequences and American music videos makes it plain by implication how strongly Demme feels that popular music has an obligation to carry a political message. These sequences alternate with scenes that not only mention various populist political trends but also cite the work of the Haitian Catholic church, which became an advocate for change after being admonished by the Pope for supporting the government's self-serving policies. When we consider that music, ritual, and grass roots political partisanship are present among the Catholic church, the island's indigenous voodoo religion, and the various musical groups we're shown, it becomes clear that in Demme's view, what is needed is a continuity among music, religion, and egalitarian politics, a point underscored through Demme's noting in the film that the majority of Haitians get their information from the radio. The implied yoking of news with music establishes a significant and, in Demme's opinion, necessary alliance.

The connections among music, politics, religion and the need for self-determination and human rights emerge in *Cousin Bobby* as well, with the added implication, present in many of Demme's fiction films and appreciable only by implication in *Haiti*, that an emphasis on the family is essential to a healthy way of life. Demme's "rediscovery" of his cousin Robert Castle, who is currently pastor of St. Mary's Episcopal Church in Harlem, makes possible an acknowledgment of one's heritage. Once this acknowledgment is reached, one realizes that one doesn't exist or, by extension, act alone—in other words, that the needs of the individual, the family, and the community are equivalent, and that a recognition of these needs should lead to political action, something that Demme achieves not only by making fiction films with social and political subtexts but also by working on documentaries that focus on contemporary issues.

Robert Castle became politically active early in his ministry; his alliance with groups such as the Black Panthers exemplifies his understanding of the need to acknowledge all oppressed people as brethren, with the resultant mandate that these beliefs then be put into practice. In Bobby's case, his political activity became so pronounced that he temporarily left the church, partially willingly, partially because he had become an embarrassment to church higher-ups.

Demme shows us the abominable conditions in Harlem, which strongly parallel those in Haiti: in both locations, decent health care, clean water, and the most basic social services are virtually nonexistent. We see that in the United States and Haiti, many people live in squalor while a minority lives in affluence. Indeed, considering the films together, one is struck by the similarities between them, with the perhaps inevitable result that the viewer begins to wonder how the deplorable conditions in either country—but perhaps especially here in this country, in which so many people are members of the middle class—could be allowed to exist. Robert Castle has a simple answer to the question implicitly raised: what we see in Harlem's deprivations is the result of long-standing institutional and national racism. It's precisely by virtue of the insistence of both *Haiti: Dreams of Democracy* and *Cousin Bobby* on justice for everyone that the films achieve their profundity and power.

Returning to a consideration of *Swimming to Cambodia* (itself, albeit only implicitly, a document on racism), you can't avoid being struck by a significant difference in the attitude of the film's "protagonist." Let's recall that there were major protests to the "secret war" in Cambodia: demonstrations, riots on American campuses. Contrasting the direct nature of these events (and those cited in *Haiti* and *Cousin Bobby*) with the incidents alluded to in *Swimming*, one becomes rather impatient with Gray's safe, passive, middle-class white reaction to some extremely objectionable political realities (this was precisely Pauline Kael's objection to the film,[7] and one can't justify Gray's attitude by saying that he is merely dramatizing this safe response; it's clear that Gray's insular, moneyed background comes back to haunt him).

Perhaps the only way to partially rescue Gray's film from the kind of condemnation justifiably leveled against it by Kael is to accept the fact that *Swimming to Cambodia* is, to appropriate documentarist Frederick Wiseman's words, a "reality fiction," that it is a stylization of empirical data.[8] Wiseman is implying by his term that in a certain sense, the only way that we can accept realities is by fictionalizing them, an effect that to a degree is caused by the very act of filming (which, however, may also tend to distance us from events).

In an important sense, Gray acts as the camera for *Swimming's* audience. Like the different lenses and film stocks used with a camera, Gray captures and adds shadings to events. What we get in *Swimming to Cambodia* are the pronouncements of a man who is acutely aware of his function as an actor, a character appearing in his own film, within his own reality fiction, with the added twist that accompanying this fiction is the greater reality fiction of *The Killing Fields*, which attempts to achieve effects similar to those of Gray's film. Perhaps it's only through the ministrative effects of films like *The Killing Fields* or *Swimming to Cambodia* that we might break out of the milieu of lies that our government promotes in order to penetrate to some sort of truth. Failing this, films dealing with politics run the risk of operating merely as entertainments.

8 | Bicentennial Babies

Every Demme film investigates American culture (and often celebrates its idiosyncratic aspects), but none places this investigation at the center of its action with the urgency of *Something Wild* (1986), from a first-time script by former NYU film student E. Max Frye. The film is Demme's most schematic, in that its plot makes obvious use of the Demme ellipsis and virtually turns its characters into prototypes; it also explores the darker side of American culture in a manner more probing than any other Demme film, even *The Silence of the Lambs*, of which it is a strong precursor.

Something Wild is also a film about the need for balance and the necessity of restoring it once it has been lost. In a comic way, the film initially characterizes the excesses of Melanie Griffith's Lulu/Audrey (predominantly her exaggerated notions of what it means to be the dark, then light-associated woman, a split also present in *Swing Shift's* pairing of Hazel and Kay), subsequently takes seriously the question of how and why these excesses came about, and then—as a result of Audrey's encounter with Charlie (Jeff Daniels)—has Audrey reconcile herself to the kind of traditional values that she seemed to be rejecting throughout the film. In doing so, *Something Wild* shows us how important to Audrey a stable and loving relationship really is, although she ultimately adopts "normalcy" in her own way. Indeed, at the film's end, Audrey strikes a nice balance between her dark tendencies (formerly emblematized in her Lulu outfit) and the goddess of whiteness that she became after she took Charlie home to her mother, where she played out the American dream of stable married life by showing off her responsible, loving "husband." At *Something Wild's* conclusion, Audrey retains this middle class attitude by appearing with a traditional symbol of white suburbia: a station wagon, although Audrey makes it characteristically hers by ensuring that it's an early model station wagon, with what looks like real wood siding, not contemporary artificial veneer. She thereby suggests that her wagon is closer to the old-time covered wagon, and that at this late point in the film she is a pioneer in new emotional territory, who's only stopped by the cafe to retrieve her man.

Yet Charlie changes too, leaving his job for a more relaxed, presumably less remunerative but, in moral and aesthetic terms, more rewarding life. Unbalanced between his desires and actions, wanting to be a sexual rebel but constrained by conventional behavior patterns, he is physically and spiritually liberated through his relationship with Audrey. The implication is that what we witness in *Something Wild* is the playing out of a characteristic Demme sexual dialectic: man meets woman, they come into conflict, they compromise, and they produce a new relationship that passes beyond the limitations of their previous relationships. *Something Wild* isn't only about the need to achieve a balance between one's private desires and one's public life; it's also about the way that the multitude of different forces in America results in a country that, perhaps because of its oddities, seems to exhibit a national character of acceptance and hope that harks back to the idealism inherent in its revolutionary beginnings. Every scene is filled with some cultural artifact: songs, road signs, beckoning highways, convenience stores, men on motorcycles (some riding in outlaw gangs, one middle-aged with a dog riding on the back of his bike). In *Something Wild*, America is in search of itself; through Charlie and Audrey—the safe (that is, harmless), middle-class white male with a suburban life and an absent wife, and the "dangerous" inner-city female—the film effects a resolution of America's contrarieties after necessarily coming to grips with the dark underside of the country's national character (it is, after all, Charlie and Audrey's meeting that makes possible the entrance of Ray [Ray Liotta] into the film, almost as though by coming together they spawned him). After *Something Wild*'s violence (which is purgative, especially in the sense that Charlie and Audrey recognize Ray as a dangerous aspect of themselves that they must confront and then somehow overcome), America, through the film's characters, emerges not only intact, but better than it was.

Involved with this aspect of the film is the fact that *Something Wild* is a road movie, that traditional American genre in which a couple (usually male, although *Thelma and Louise*, taking its cue from Michelle DeVille's *Voyage En Douce*, has applied the genre's attributes to women), in the process of journeying along the nation's highways, replay the Huck Finn and Jim river voyage by trying to understand themselves through a confrontation with American culture.[1] Like the couples in important American road movies such as *Scare-*

Something Wild's balanced couples: Lulu and Charlie (*top*) and Ray and Audrey (*bottom*)

crow and *Thunderbolt and Lightfoot*, *Something Wild*'s duo reach the outermost point of their journey and find those powerful forces of violence and death (here in the person of Ray) that American society tries to either deny or suppress.[2] The twist in *Something Wild* is that destructiveness isn't left behind after it is encountered; it comes home to suburbia, crashing through the window of Charlie's house when he least expects it. The implication is that, once unleashed, dark forces, like some evil genie, can't be easily placed back in the bottle; indeed, these forces not only cannot be rebottled, they must be directly confronted and, in this case, overcome.

At least at first, Charlie is a lily-white, predominantly law-abiding individual, and Lulu an apparent rebel who likes to toy with danger (Lulu uses her handcuffs in a little game; Ray uses them to subdue Charlie so that he can brutalize Audrey). If early in the film Charlie seems to represent white culture and repression, Lulu represents Third World cultures and liberation. Yet her appearance is mostly a ruse—intentionally exaggerated clothes, overabundance of jewelry, artificially colored hair. At the film's beginning, each one of the characters is wearing a costume and a mask of behavior. Through his excessive, uncompromising behavior, Ray, the dark catalyst, strips these facades away, and makes Audrey want to protect Charlie, and Charlie want to save Audrey.

Lulu tests Charlie repeatedly, as though he were a knight vying for her favors, to see if he is worthy of her (thus underscoring the film's romantic subtext, which also makes possible *Something Wild*'s stereotypes of good and evil, a carryover from *Fighting Mad*). Charlie succeeds each time, lying his way out of dilemmas, even going so far as to use Lulu's handcuffs (with which she bound Charlie in the midst of what she incorrectly considered an adulterous liaison) and (inadvertently) Ray's knife against Ray at the film's end, actions complemented by Audrey's using one of Charlie's symbols of white, law-abiding suburbia, his golf clubs, against Ray. In other words, Ray is executed by instruments of both antipodes of American culture: its violent part and its safe part. Having offended the order of good karmic behavior in which Demme believes, Ray dies for his behavior.

Although Lulu calls Charlie a good liar (after he has talked his way out of trouble during a potentially compromising phone conversation with his boss), what both characters are actually moving toward through their relationship is the truth about each other. Charlie is neither the repressed organization man nor the liberated individual he seems at the dance before Ray appears. Lulu is neither the dark, black-helmeted Louise Brooks/Pandora's box[3] of evil that she seems at

Something Wild's beginning nor the spun blonde, all-light Audrey of its middle section. They're each a little bit of both modes, but mostly they're lonely people, the one abandoned by his wife, the other having abandoned her husband (whom she must at some time have loved), both of whom want affection and stability, along with enough spontaneity to make life interesting. Audrey can't find what she needs in Ray, who was obviously too dangerous for her; Charlie couldn't find what he needed in his wife, for whom he may have seemed too tame. Through Charlie's touching phone call with his son, when he tells the boy to "knock one out of the park for [him]," Demme shows us that Charlie is a very caring man. Similarly, in front of her mother, Audrey spins a tale about the traditional domestic bliss that she and Charlie have which reveals how much she wants the kind of affection and approval that one can only get from one's parents. The two are a perfect pair: Charlie with a child but no family; Audrey with a family (her mother) but no child. Like *Married to the Mob*'s Mike and Angela, united, Charlie and Audrey constitute a whole.

The degree of pleasure that we derive from *Something Wild* is in no small part a function of the way that the film reveals its machinery blatantly, showing us much more obviously than in any other Demme film how the ellipsis operates (in this case, with the exit from New York, the encounter with evil at the end point of Charlie and Audrey's journey, and then a return to New York), and how the characters mesh with each other and fulfill each other's needs. What results from watching *Something Wild* is an awareness of the film as both a series of believable realities and as a fiction, a duality of consciousness that complements the film's duality of action (a two-way trip out of town and back, thereby setting up the clash between *Something Wild*'s urban beginning and its predominantly rural Pennsylvania and Virginia interludes; two store robberies; two motel stops; two changes of clothes for Charlie) and character (two Audreys; two versions of Charlie: passive victim and active avenger; two versions of Ray: nice guy and killer).

Like many of Demme's characters, at their film's beginning Charlie and Audrey seem to be living out a fantasy with each other: Charlie plays the role of married innocent, Audrey plays the role of temptress. What is fascinating to watch is that when Charlie and Audrey really start to fall in love with each other at the dance, Charlie starts acting like more of a free spirit than he had before. He goes off for a drive in the night in a dark car and starts drinking (something to which he had at first objected when he had seen Lulu doing it) just when Lulu, having turned sweet and innocent (a quality emblematized by the white dress that she wears to the reunion), is compelled because of Ray's reappearance to become distant and guarded, and can only watch while she and her lover are whisked off on some terrible journey. As the wife of one of Charlie's coworkers says, "He's gonna get in trouble with those guys." But it's not just the kind of trouble that comes from driving a stolen car or robbing a convenience store, things that Ray does in the film. It's the kind of trouble that results when you've tapped into the dark part of the human psyche and unleashed all of the forces hiding there, among them repressed attitudes concerning sex and conformity. Unchecked, these impulses go wild. This aspect is already prevalent when Ray for no reason pistol whips the clerk during the robbery at the convenience store,[4] and recurs at his motel room when he gets into a shouting match with a man next door, during which Ray kicks a hole in the wall. Once begun, this alienating violence escalates, becomes aphrodisiac in effect, and is difficult to restrain.

As the characters' behavior changes, so too does the way that they feel about their appearance. We've already seen Lulu transform herself into Audrey at her mother's house. By the time that Ray has stolen Audrey away, Charlie has also changed his attitude about his looks. In the Virginia convenience store, the normally self-conscious Charlie is so intent on rescuing Audrey that he undresses right out in the open. By this point in the film, Charlie isn't concerned about his bloody shirt either, or his physical injuries; in his damn-it-all attitude, he begins to resemble his dark counterpart, Ray, even repeating verbatim Ray's line about how a "broken nose ain't gonna kill ya." He's jettisoned fastidiousness because all that he cares about is what is most important: helping Audrey escape from Ray. At the same time as Charlie is beginning to emulate Ray, Ray is beginning to mirror Charlie's actions, evidencing the kind of methodical behavior (for example, tracking down Charlie and Audrey in New York) that Charlie had exhibited when following Ray and Audrey. The difference in motivation is significant, though. Ray is out for revenge. He doesn't just want to get Audrey back, as does Charlie; he also wants to punish Charlie. Charlie acts to recover Audrey in response to his more tender feelings, while Ray acts on feelings stemming from pain and rejection.

Audrey seems to have prepared the way for Charlie's chivalric behavior by her own restrained, coquettish behavior, especially when she's with her mother. Although she reverts to outlandishness at the prom by revealing to one of Charlie's amazed coworkers (who is married to one of Audrey's old schoolmates) that she and Charlie are lovers, it's clear that Audrey does this because Charlie had just previously pushed her out of the way when he had seen this man, as though she didn't mean anything to Charlie and was merely an embarrassment. When Charlie and Audrey are in their most conventional incarnation, as a pair of wounded people, Ray is quick to go for their jugulars, making fun of them, telling them that they look like a couple on television, which in a sense they do—for surely they are trying to resemble those culturally archetypal, well-scrubbed white couples one sees in traditional situation comedies and light dramatic series.

But Ray is predominantly wrong. By this point in the film, Charlie and Audrey have a genuine affection for each other; they're two adults who have somehow been swept up by the feelings of love and innocence that can occur at a high school reunion. Magically, they have gained access to the one pure desire in America, which dates from the 1776 act of rebellion: the need for an independent identity, an impulse that this reunion, which is being held for the class of 1976 and which bills itself as the "Spirit of '76 revisited" is, perhaps unintentionally, celebrating. Yet just as in 1776, there are dangerous forces at work here too; the 1776ers were frightened of the Indians and the threat of the dark forest, reactions that can be seen as conceptually necessary to the completion of the classic romantic paradigm of good and evil that is at work in American cultural history, of which *Something Wild* is so representative an example. The appearance of Ray, coming as it does at the height of Charlie and Audrey's demonstrated devotion to each other—after the courtship dances that the two have gone through, which take place in front of a large American flag—makes it plain that Ray is a force that Charlie and Audrey must confront if their relationship is to have any validity.

Ray can't understand the innocent feelings that Charlie and Audrey are experiencing because all that he has ever felt is anger and frustration. He's apparently never been at peace long enough to enjoy his life. As we learn from the newspaper clippings in Audrey's scrapbook, Ray was in trouble even before he left high school; perhaps he came from a reckless and abusive family. But all that we can do is guess at Ray's background. Unlike Charlie and Audrey, Ray is at best a sketch of a character, far more of a romantic prototype of evil than a real human being, although in one sense this characteristic benefits the film as well, since it makes Ray more mysterious, and his violence therefore more ominous. We don't know where Ray's rage comes from; consequently, when it erupts, it's much more frightening because it seems inexplicable. Ray is not only unpredictable, wild, and lawless (traits appropriated by Lulu); even worse, he despises order and culture and affinity with any group. He's a textbook social deviant. In Charles Willeford's *Sideswipe*, Troy Louden, the book's sociopath character, says of himself, "I'm a professional criminal, what the shrinks call a criminal psychopath. What it means is, I know the difference between right and wrong and all that, but I don't give a shit. . . . If I see the right thing to do and want to do it, I do it, and if I see the wrong thing and want to do it, I do that, too."[5] The description fits Ray perfectly.

Ray can't accept the fact that Audrey is no longer the woman who found him attractive or loved him; thus his comment when he discovers Audrey's handcuffs. Chuckling to himself in a self-congratulatory way, he says, "Old habits die hard, eh baby?" It's almost as though at this point, the handcuffs are a symbol of Ray, not just of his criminal background but of the fact that by virtue of his upbringing, he's handcuffed to an underworld milieu.[6] Ray would doubtless subscribe to the view that people are meant to be what they become, that they are products of the social forces acting upon them, which limit and, to a degree, govern the choices that we make in life. (Once again, Willeford's work comes into play here, as when *Sideswipe*'s Troy refers to Jack Black's autobiography *You Can't Win*, which is a testament to fate).[7] And though *Something Wild* is somewhat unfair to Ray, condemning him for who he is despite the fact that he doesn't seem to have much capability of changing, the film's morality mandates that he reap the consequences of his negative karma, which to a great extent is a function of the bad choices that he has made in his life. When the evil forces that Ray unleashes come back around to him, he dies. As Charlie tells Ray, "Violence never solved anything; what goes around comes around. You're gonna learn that some day." Ray thinks that this is nonsense, and we might be inclined to agree with him, ascribing such platitudes to Charlie's naiveté, were it not that the phrase's meaning, and the satisfying elliptical moral structure that it implies, are endemic to Demme's work, and are borne out by the film's plot.

Demme's ellipsis not only invokes a karmic view of the universe, but also tells us that we are supposed to have learned something on our road journeys that should be applied on our subsequent go-around in life, so that we can do better the next time. (The concept of the road journey fits in well with the film's karmic view, since in Asian culture the wisdom of the Tao—the road or the way—is often sought through a pilgrimage into the countryside.) Perhaps more so than any other Demme film, *Something Wild* shows us its director's faith that change will be for the better—that the good will flourish and the bad will be punished (which is why, as we'll see, the black comedy twist ending in *The Silence of the Lambs* is so inappropriate and disappointing).

Although there is choice in *Something Wild*, there are also cosmic and comic coincidences. Charlie is in the New York luncheonette at just the right time to be seen by Lulu; the police just happen to come into the Virginia restaurant when Charlie needs them to reinforce his confrontation with Ray; the young blonde woman just happens to pass by the restaurant window when Ray needs money to pay the check that Charlie leaves him. And yet the characters are very free, too. Audrey plans to go to the high school reunion; Ray plans to be there to look for her; and Charlie carefully plans his moves after Ray and Audrey disappear together. What *is* beyond the characters' control, though, is the clash between light and dark elements that they unleash as a result of their actions.

When Charlie meets Audrey and drives off with her out of New York, they're doing more than simply leaving a metropolis; they're also beginning to effect a change in themselves from naiveté into knowledge, moving toward a greater understanding of themselves and other people. But they need the presence of Ray to do it. Charlie and Audrey *have to* "get in trouble with those guys" in order to divest themselves of the masks that they are wearing as substitutes for their real selves.[8] By the film's end, after their assumed personae have disappeared, Charlie and Audrey are each far more like the wild (untamed by society's ridiculous demands) things that they want to be; sex and love have transformed them.

Although it might be true for some people that (as a rural sage tells Charlie outside the motel where he and Audrey are staying) "it's better to be a live dog than a dead lion," this conventional wisdom[9] is based on practicality at the expense of daring, and really doesn't pertain to the way that Charlie acts. If he had wanted to be a live dog, Charlie would have remained the whipped cur he was when he left Ray's motel room. Instead, lion-like, Charlie tracks Ray through Virginia and takes Audrey away from him.

There's more to Charlie's question to Audrey just before they enter the reunion than might at first appear. "Who am I supposed to be?"[10] he asks, and when he gets the answer, he quite creatively enters into the fiction of being married to Audrey, yet not to the degree that Audrey does. While Audrey maintains the charade throughout their visit to her home state, Charlie earlier admits to Audrey's mother, Peaches, that they're only pretending. "I just met her recently," he confesses. In her way, Audrey is far more prone to fantasy than is Charlie. Indeed, it's Charlie's more realistic and practical side, coupled with his romantic desire to liberate his woman from the clutches of the dark dragon, that makes it possible for him to get Audrey away from Ray.

Audrey is right about Charlie: he's a "real nice guy, maybe a little too nice." But then again, maybe he's not so nice, at least not in the way that Audrey intends the word to be understood. Charlie isn't harmless; he's a fighter. He contends with Ray twice, once in the Virginia restaurant, once at Charlie's home, and bests Ray each time. In the restaurant, Charlie has Ray caught between silence and exposure, so that Ray is figuratively handcuffed by circumstances. At his house, Charlie is himself handcuffed, literally, yet he turns the handcuffs against Ray, choking him with them. Ray is such a violent force that Charlie needs help in subduing Ray, yet he wins nonetheless, and that's what is important. At first, Audrey's statement to Charlie at his Stony Brook home about seeing his "other half" (apparently, she's referring to his suburban white lifestyle) is left hanging as a cliché, but then the statement is exploded: what Audrey really means is the other half of Charlie's personality, the part that can fight for her and still be tender and loving. Charlie thereby exhibits a balance of aggression and compassion that someone like Ray could never achieve.

Yet Charlie is no murderer. Even when he's choking Ray with the handcuffs we know that we couldn't accept Charlie as a killer—not even one who killed in self-defense. Appropriately impaled on his own knife, Ray in effect kills himself. We are spared the cinematic convention of his dying scene. After Ray is stabbed, he looks at himself in the mirror (as so many of Demme's characters do), with no suggestion of any gained self-knowledge about the end to which all of his violence has brought him. We merely see him repeat his characteristic gesture of running his fingers through his hair, which this time leave a blood stain on his forehead; he then stumbles off down the hall, the cleats on the front and back of his shit-kicking boots shining along the carpet. Through Ray's death we see the sacrifice of Charlie's final illusion about protection from life's painful qualities: that the suburbs are safe. As Ray makes Charlie see, you're not safe from evil anywhere—that is, unless you've first met and conquered evil in yourself. This is the unintentional office that Ray performs for Charlie. After he's stabbed, Ray says, "Shit, Charlie," as though what has happened wasn't absolutely necessary. To the end, then, Ray fails to realize that his own violence must travel full circle and kill him. At the scene's conclusion, the surviving couple are reduced to their most basic reactions: Charlie can only stare, Audrey can only cry.

At *Something Wild*'s end, Charlie goes looking for Audrey (improbably, he has lost track of her). In the process of searching, he sees that the city is still full of bad karma. The woman who now occupies Audrey's apartment tells Charlie that she thinks her landlord is "screwing'' her on her rent (the term's ambiguity reinvokes the film's concern with the continuity between sexual and supposedly non-sexual behavior); Charlie says he isn't surprised. We then return to the luncheonette outside of which Charlie and Lulu first met. The same man, with the same coworker beside him, is once again talking across the counter to a customer; the same waitress who brought Charlie his check at the film's beginning does so again. It's as though during the film's preceding events, Charlie and Audrey had passed out of time into a mystical realm in which they've had a religious experience, a confrontation, like the one experienced by Arjuna in the *Bhagavad Gita*, with absolute good and evil.

But there *are* differences: this time, Charlie leaves the money for his check although, as before, a kind of theft nonetheless takes place. When Audrey miraculously appears outside the luncheonette, she is wearing a black and white polka dot dress, which shows that she has resolved her contradictory impulses, a resolution mirrored in the black and white checkered pattern of Charlie's shirt. Audrey brings the film's circle to a close; as at *Something Wild*'s beginning, she offers Charlie a ride, although there's still a bit of the rebel in her, as is plain from the fact that her station wagon is illegally parked near a fire hydrant. Liberated from his restrictive corporate job, Charlie is now ready to join her, both of them free to express affection and fun when it strikes them. They've been reborn into a more honest world in which they can meet all of life's joys and sorrows head on, but together, in love, which, as Demme convinces us via the film's spirit and structure, is the way that it was always meant to be.

9 | The Gang's All Here

Demme has said that the story of *Married to the Mob* (1988) is so light that the film almost floats away.[1] Yet despite this quality, *Married* is a seriously upbeat film. Much of this effect has to do with the comic tone that Demme sustains throughout. The director was immediately attracted to the script, by Barry Strugatz and Mark R. Burns, which turns the gangster film genre on its head by focusing on mob wife Angela de Marco (Michelle Pfeiffer) instead of the usual macho goings-on. Demme's typical upright young man is Matthew Modine, as Mike Downey of the FBI, who is out to get mob boss Tony Russo (Dean Stockwell) but who becomes more interested in Angela.

As he did in *Something Wild*, Demme relies heavily on music, with a score by David Byrne and songs by Sinead O'Connor and Chris Isaak, among others, that help keep the action moving. Inside jokes—audience recognition of actors like Al Lewis ("Grandpa Munster") or musicians like David Johansen—function along with Demme's use of colorful street characters to keep the frame interesting. And of course, Demme's stock actors pop up, supplemented by members of the production company (producer Kenneth Utt appears as an FBI agent; music supervisor Gary Goetzman, as a piano player).

The film's whimsical tone carries over to the behavior of its gangster characters, whose world, like the film's, is abstracted. The men are all known by ridiculous nicknames, most of which either refer to animals (Tony the Tiger, Nick the Snake, Vinnie the Slug, Al the Worm) or phallic vegetables (Cucumber Frank de Marco). And though the inside of Tony's house seems middle-class bland, the same can't be said for the inside of Frank (Alec Baldwin) and Angela's house, which is filled with microwaves, VCRs, and televisions (many of them in their original boxes), as well as an outdoor lamp post and a terrible couch. The style is suburbia gone mad rococo. Although Angela's main objection is to the immorality of her and Frank's lifestyle (she complains at

Frank and the unhappy Angela

one point, "everything we own, everything we wear, everything we eat fell off of a truck"), it's clear that she also feels smothered by the middle-class claustrophobia of it all, the overt consumerism that's meant to distract her from the objectionable nature of Frank's activities, the mob wives' pointless trips to the hairstylist, and the card games that the women play while the men have confabs about whom they're going to kill next.

The world in which the film's gangsters live is also an exaggerated, escapist one, characterized not only by visits to a nightclub as mock castle (does Tony see himself as the royal head of the gang?) where the waitresses dress in outfits that mimic those worn by ladies in waiting, but also by a devout faith in material objects. These men firmly believe that happiness derives from buying things and wielding power. Like *The Godfather*'s Corleones, the Russo family measures success by money, manipulation, and mastication. Indeed, how well one eats is extremely important: thus the obsession of Tony's driver Tommy (Paul Lazar) with discussing food, an activity in which he is engaged just before he and Frank kill a man on a train. The juxtaposition of eating and furious action, both self-indulgent activities on which the gang members seem to thrive, recalls *The Godfather*'s Clemenza who, after Paulie's murder, tells his henchman to make sure to retrieve the cannoli from the death car.

Like Frank, Tony is a consummate consumer, although, comically, he reveals his lack of good taste through his addiction to the fast food at Burger World, a corporate entity, much like the mob of which Tony is the head. Unlike the usual cinematic Mafioso, he seems to spurn Italian food in favor of American junk. "It's a Burger World town," the restaurant's theme song says. Indeed, for Tony and Tommy and the rest of their gang, it's a Burger World universe, characterized by the moral shallowness of garish colors (especially prevalent at Burger World and the nightclub where Tony's gang congregates, the latter of which is bathed in a hellish red light), available women, ridiculous nicknames, gangster-style tough-guy dialogue, and double crosses.

The irony, of course, is that these men don't see that their various rendezvous in "Theme Rooms" at the Fantasia hotel (which oxymoronically advertises in large back-lit letters, "Discreet Entrance") are just another part of their Disney World version of gangsterism, and that they aren't gangsters so much as parodies of gangsters—if anything, parodies of parodies, since traditional movie gangsters are themselves prone to the use of clichés (as Humphrey Bogart's gangster says in *Dead End* when he's dying, "Get back; I'm going out"). These men are living in a dream world of fast women and shoot-em-ups.

Demme has this self-deceptive dreaminess inhere in another world as well: that of the mob's mirror-image counterpart, the FBI. Unable to reform one of the mob, her husband, Angela inadvertently manages to humanize an already quirky individual, Mike, bringing him over into a third world, one influenced strongly by Latino and reggae culture.

But other people in the film are trapped in fantasies, too. Tony's wife Connie (Mercedes Ruehl) is strongly dependent on her marriage; when she catches Tony in an apparent liaison with Angela, she says in typical soap opera dialogue that she has "nothing to live for"; Tony's response to this statement (he tells her to think of her credit cards and her game shows) is a litany to petty reasons for Connie's not killing herself. Opposed to this universe is the vibrant, honest one of the Lower East Side, where the implication is that happiness has nothing to do with money, a generalization that Demme makes convincing through the attractive character traits of the people, chiefly Rita ("Sister" Carol East), whom Angela meets down there.

Although Demme's whimsical tone has the unfortunate side-effect of diminishing the impact that the film's murders should have on us, there is an exception to this response: just before Tommy—whose gentle looks and humorous devotion to food endear him to us—is shot, when he tells the gunman/cashier at Burger World, "Don't." Aside from this point, we don't emotionally react when anyone in the film is killed. Demme can't have us enjoy the film's light tone and avoid distancing us from the film's murders, since all of these activities are taking place in the same universe; and though the director regrets this effect,[2] we don't think he needs to. The possibility of Angela's being given a second chance at a better life seems so moving that it more than redeems the drawbacks that the film's lighthearted tone may have. Indeed, the scene in which Mike talks to Angela and they hold each other all through the night without making love is surely one of the most affecting love scenes in all of movies, and represents the culmination of a change that Angela catalyzes in Mike, who earlier had the potential for seeing through the bureau's harshness and had begun to believe that Angela wasn't the mob dupe/tootsie that he had initially assumed she was.

One of the ways that Demme distances us from the film's violence is through his use of music. *Married to the Mob* begins with the murder of a man on a train whom Tommy and Frank kill by shooting him through the head. This death would certainly seem to us far more upsetting were it not that just as we see the results of the shooting, Demme blends in an upbeat piece of music ("Bizarre Love Triangle") that not only abstracts the murder and keeps the film's pacing lively, but also provides a segue into the next scene. In essence, our lack of reaction mirrors that of Tommy and Frank, who get off the train complaining about a particularly mundane matter: how crowded it is, and what fools commuters are for riding trains like this one every day. They not only don't feel bad about the shooting, they feel superior to the kinds of people riding the train, even though Tommy and Frank in their way are just as traditional as the commuters whom they're condemning.

At the beauty parlor, Angela is having her hair done; judging by the glum look on her face (she seems very far away, lost in depressing thoughts) it's almost as though Angela has taken on herself the remorse that she might very well feel her husband should be experiencing. Indeed, she knows that killing is one of the ways that Frank advances in the mob. During a later argument between the two, Frank asks, "How am I supposed to get ahead in the family?" Angela sarcastically replies, "Same way you always have: lie, cheat, steal, kill." It's a way of life from which Angela finds it difficult to escape.

Although Angela spurns the friendly advances of the mob wives as a way of trying to disentangle herself from the actions of their hus-

Tony and Angela

bands, it's plain that this is at best a halfway measure. What Angela needs is a deus ex machina miracle to deliver her from the spiderweb of death and deception in which she finds herself (to her dismay, even her son Joey [Anthony J. Nili] becomes involved in deceit, as in the cheating hustle of the three card monte game that he and Tony Jr. [Jason Allen] play against some neighborhood kids, and in the way that Tony tries to buy Joey's affection with money and gifts). Yet the threat of the family against Angela is always present. As Connie tells her in a line whose meaning is later echoed by Tony when he comes to Angela's Lower East Side apartment after she's abandoned her suburban home, "We're your friends" (Tony says "family"), both of them communicating to Angela the ominousness inherent in the statement, which Connie states directly: "whether you like it or not."

In *Married to the Mob* there are two kinds of family life: oppressive and supportive. The mob families represent a threat to Angela's attempt to create a moral atmosphere in which to raise her son. As for Tony, what should be the loving ambience of his wife's birthday party is compromised by two of Tony's henchmen arriving with news about the whereabouts of the recently departed Angela, on whom Tony has sexual designs. Tony's disloyalty to Connie is also exemplified by his extramarital affairs, two of which we see; neither one is based on any trust. Thus, the kiss-of-death necklace that Tony gives to Angela not only signals his awareness of duplicity on Angela's part, but is the identical necklace that he had given to Karen Lutnick and retrieved after shooting Karen for sleeping with Frank.

Connie's relationships with her friends are very similar to the kinds of relationships that Tony has with his subordinates; they're marked by power on the part of the Russos and obeisance on everyone else's. Yet Connie and Tony are not that secure about their power, since neither one of them can tolerate rejection. Indeed, when Angela spurns Connie and Tony's overtures of friendship, they become hostile, albeit in different ways. Connie is first angry; when spurned in the beauty parlor, she says of Angela to her other woman friends, "That bitch; she thinks her shit don't stink." Tony assaults the protesting Angela on the day of Frank's funeral, when she is most vulnerable. Death, sex, and, especially, women in extremely vulnerable situations seem to excite him (thus his involvement not only with Angela but with Karen, who couldn't publicly acknowledge her relationship with Tony and whom he saw at his convenience).

In fact, all of Tony's relationships (especially those with women) are pathological; through them, Demme shows us that relationships based on inequality of power are wrong, an aspect Mike inadvertently underscores when, talking of Tony, he mentions that he seems to have a strange fear of Connie. We see this fear in operation twice when Connie, wielding a gun, places Tony's sexual prowess in jeopardy. The fact that Connie threatens Tony's masculinity each time, the second time in a dream sequence, when Tony's genitals are exposed (he's been urinating), shows how sexually based Tony's insecurity is, demonstrating quite clearly that Tony's aggressive behavior with women (as well as his mob behavior with men) and all of his gun-play are overcompensations for a weak sense of self. Nonetheless, Tony courts Angela, characteristically doing so by using money and material objects to try to win her over. His gift card may say, "Because I care," but Angela knows better: this is a man who is incapable of caring, who can only aggressively possess a woman, never share something with her. Indeed, the only character with whom Tony shows a modicum of real affection is Tommy; yet after Tommy dies, the best that Tony can come up with in the way of a response is a mild statement of pity. The manner in which Tony verbalizes his regret, and the fact that it is expressed in the same tone as his regret about Frank, whom he didn't mind killing and whose death he does not mourn, makes it pretty obvious that he isn't exactly grieving about Tommy's death either. "Yeah," Tony says in response to Angela's condoling statement about his driver. "First Frankie, now Tommy."

There is a pronounced lack of affect among these men, a reflection of their sterile, self-deceptive way of life. By contrast, Angela, who's in touch with her feelings, seems to be a very emotional woman (Michelle Pfeiffer communicates Angela's grief over her lifestyle quite well in the argument scene with Frank: her eyes seem bloodshot even before she starts to cry). It's clear that Angela wants someone to care for her and for whom she can care without any conditions being placed on her love. The unfortunate irony of *Married to the Mob*'s middle section is that Angela is clearly falling in love with Mike, a feeling that Mike, because of his initial view that Angela conspired her husband's death with Tony, at first resists reciprocating. Yet as is typical not only in Demme's films but also in myth, the redemptive woman transforms the man, bringing him to a more humanistic and loving state. Mike starts out as little more than a jerk, just like his regional director, Franklin (Trey Wilson). Initially, Mike's a wise guy (like Tony) who speaks in bitter metaphors ("Karen Lutnick was a real dish; Tony finds out Frank's eating off his plate"). And when he proposes the surveillance scenario involving Angela to Franklin, he does so in the crudest terms. "I say we tap her phone, her house, her bedroom, stake her out, scope her, tail her coming and going, in and out, and we catch Tony Russo with his pants down." "Sounds good," Franklin says. "Get the bitch." It's not "get Tony," it's "get Angela." Like the mob, the FBI seems to direct its hostility against women.

Mike is obviously looking for advancement in this objectionable organization. "Bingo" he says with delight more than once to his partner Benitez (Oliver Platt) when they see things going their way; and when they're apart, Benitez virtually licks his chops over how well their sting operation is going. "Woof, woof, woof" Benitez says at one point. "Promotion in this for the both of us." Yet Mike is puzzled: Angela's activities—giving up her house, moving to downtown New York, looking for a job—don't fit the pattern of ruthless, scheming behavior that he expects. Mike remarks in a statement that reveals his underlying morality, "She seems so nice." Benitez can't see this quality, though (ultimately, neither can Franklin). "Huh?" Benitez responds. Even after Angela's heartfelt confession to Mike that her husband was a member of the Russo crime family, was killed in a mob hit, and that she hates the mob's members, male and female, Mike still fails to communicate this knowledge to Franklin. Mike may tell Benitez that they've "treed the wrong possum" but we never see him say anything to Franklin about his discovery; perhaps because it involves an emotional truth, he suspects that Franklin wouldn't understand.

Benitez accuses Mike of getting involved with Angela only because "your little sausage [got] lonely," and Franklin's view of Mike's involvement is no less crude. "You're thinking with your dick," he tells him. Yet the statements reveal how corrupt Benitez and Franklin's views of relationships are. To them, as to Tony and Frank and, doubtless, the rest of the gang, there are no tender feelings; there's only sex. And if there is sex, it's not the expression of emotion but simply the lust for physical gratification, control, and domination. Mike's affection for Angela involves him in a language of communication that neither the mob nor the men of the FBI can understand. The reciprocity between criminals and law enforcers is expressed in such a way that it seems like a joke, even though what's being asserted constitutes a serious political and social comment about conventional government and law enforcement agencies and their corruption. "You people work just like the mob," Angela says in response to Franklin's threats of imprisonment and the loss of her child. When Franklin replies to Angela, "Oh, there's a big difference, Mrs. de Marco. The mob is run by murdering, thieving, lying, cheating psychopaths; we work for the president of the United States of America," the line gets the biggest laugh of any in the whole film, mostly because Demme makes us realize that Franklin can't see the truth: that the president in many ways is living the same kind of exploitative, manipulative life as Tony Russo—and he's as much of a small-time hood as Tony as well.

Mike, though, is not quite a representative FBI man; indeed, a conflict between his FBI and humane aspects develops in him as soon as he touches Angela, when he's giving her a foot massage. Intimate contact with another human being brings out Mike's emotional side, the part that knows that there's something wrong with the mechanistic, unfeeling FBI philosophy but which can't seem to pinpoint it. Mike realizes as well that Angela doesn't know that it was Tony who killed Frank, and comes to appreciate what a terrible position she is in, not only pursued sexually by a mobster but also, unbeknownst to her, by the mobster who killed her husband.

Angela is a strong woman, although she doesn't realize this until moving to the Lower East Side after her husband's death. After a disappointing day of job hunting (a task at which she does not seem very experienced), and voyeuristic victimization at the hands of the Chicken Lickin' manager (Tracey Walter)—whose Russo-like obsession with power is expressed by the sign on his desk that reads, "Yield to the boss"—she is then rudely invaded by Tony and Tommy in the one place where she might have felt safe: her apartment. When Angela is alone on the street after getting Tony and Tommy to leave, though, good fortune puts her in the right spot at the right time, something that often happens in Demme's films (as in *Melvin and Howard*, when Melvin meets "Hughes," and *Something Wild*, when Charlie meets Audrey). Angela notices the "Help Wanted" sign in the window of Rita's shop (a proletarian version of the beauty parlor we'd seen her in before). By the time she approaches Hello Gorgeous, Angela is very near defeat. Yet as Pfeiffer plays her, Angela is still able to muster enough confidence to straighten up, square her shoulders with determination, and walk into the shop. She asks for the job, honestly states her limited qualifications, says she'll do any kind of work—cleaning, answering phones—doesn't even ask to cut hair (thereby indicating her lack of snobbery), and then reveals a bit of her vulnerability by saying to Rita, "Please?" and moving her head up and down as though to say, "Come on; give me a chance." She gets the job because of her attitude of willful humility—and maybe also because she looks nuts enough in her Chicken Lickin' outfit, which Rita stares at for a few seconds with a cocked head, to fit right into this counterculture establishment.

Everyone has similar bits of business that humanize even the most corrupt of them. Tony and Tommy don't just like the food at Burger World; they also share an inexplicable fondness for the Burger World theme song. For all of his duplicity, Frank seems quirky by virtue of his inability to realize that the interior of his house is an eyesore ("When I look at this house you know what I see? I see a swell house full of beautiful furnishings," Frank says; he fails to realize how wrong things are even after Angela asks him "Don't you get it? Everything has blood on it"). Al and Nick are distinguished by their playful interaction with one another and, in a somewhat gruesome way, even with Mike (after he is shot by Mike at the film's end, Nick says, "Gee, Mike, ya didn't have to do that").

Connie stands out by virtue of her loudmouthed attitude, evident when her plane is taxiing into Miami and Connie, getting her bag from the overhead compartment, says to the stewardess who asks her to remain in her seat, "Honey, forget about it," after which Connie topples over backwards. She also has a toughness in contention with her blindness to the ludicrous nature of her outfits, such as the one with the multiple pelts that she wears to the airport (when she runs toward Tony, the pelts go flying every which way), although Tony's outfit in the scene—white topcoat, white suit, dark glasses, beige fedora—is no less absurd, a travesty of the typical gangster look. They're all comic book characters. Even Benitez seems endearing, playing with an Etch-A-Sketch while monitoring the hidden microphones in Angela's apartment, rising up with a delightfully puzzled look on his face after Mike finishes his explanation to Joey about how long ago the dinosaurs really lived (it looks as though Benitez is going to have to go home and think about that one for a while). Before we know that underneath all of his FBI rhetoric he's really a nice guy, Mike is early on characterized by his silly dressing device, as well as by the automatic cat feeder that he uses.

Only Mike and Angela seem genuine, though. They're pet devotees as well, an important quality in Demme's films since it indicates the need for expressing love and receiving it[3] (although Mike's genuine liking for cats also seems linked to FBI stealth, as well as to the big-cat aspect of his prey: Tony the Tiger). Mike and Angela are fated lovers meant for something better. And it's precisely that "something better" that Angela wants for her son. Joey has already been corrupted by exposure to Frank; he knows where his father's gun is and plays at shooting it, just as he takes to the laser tag game that sharpshooter Tony Russo—who twirled his gun Wild West style after he shot Frank, and who uses a two-gun shooting technique during the Burger World ambush—had given him.[4] Yet the kid is still an innocent at heart. When he says about Angela's decrepit East Side apartment that he'll stay there with his mother but that "this place really sucks," you can see that Joey is street smart but honest. It's that latter quality in him (brought to the fore when Joey and Angela part at the school and the two touch fingers à la E.T. and tell each other to "b-e-e-e g-o-o-o-d") that Angela wants to protect.

Angela has a simple desire: she wants to "lead a good life, a life we [she and Joey] can be proud of," and fortunately, it looks like she will be able to do so. The neighborhood she moves into is precisely the kind of location where she can find the opportunity to start life over. Mike's statement to Angela in this respect is very touching, and worth quoting in full. "It's not easy to turn your life around, especially when your past keeps coming back to haunt you. . . . We all make mistakes. The important thing is to realize it and to do something about it and to let yourself off the hook, because everybody deserves a second chance—especially someone like you."

The Lower East Side seems to be a place where people have a good time and accept you for what you are. It's a neighborhood that affirms life. The contrast between the place's lively aspects and the death orientation of the gangster world (which is linked with the sterility of mass culture) is made plain during the latino dance club sequence, which takes place simultaneously with the "Hamburger Homicide" at Burger World.[5] The ominous music accompanying the shootout blends into and contends with the music to which Mike and Angela are dancing, with total abandon on Angela's part and even a bit

Mike and Angela's dance club date

of abandon on Mike's (who nonetheless never forgets that he's on assignment).

When Angela meets Mike, she reacts with a combination of
coquettish shyness and a sense of abandon. Back at her apartment
after the dance, and carried away by the genuine affection that she's
feeling for Mike (Angela is seriously interested in Mike, not just playing at romance as the Russos, Benitez, and Mike [initially] interpret
her actions), Angela changes into a robe, turns down the lights,
suggests that they get more comfortable, and asks Mike to massage
her feet.

The slight twist early on, though, is that at first, Mike is trying
to exploit Angela, just as Tony is attempting to do. When Mike and
Angela are in her apartment building elevator together, the distinction
between the two characters is emblematized by the chair between
them, whose rungs separate Mike from Angela as though Angela were
imprisoned (later, in a presentiment of things to come, Angela will be
carrying the chair down the hall in such a way so that, in a foreshad-
owing of Tony's final incarceration, we see him behind its bar-like
rungs). Yet it's not so much that Mike and Angela are on opposite sides
of the law as that at this point they're at moral antipodes: Mike merely
wants to use Angela to get to Tony, whereas Angela is beginning to fall
in love with Mike. Together, they make an ideal pair, but a bit of a
change in Mike is necessary first.

The end point of this change occurs in Miami when Mike realizes during the sting operation against Tony that he really loves Angela. "What are you doing here, Dog Face?" Connie asks Mike after she enters Tony's suite. Mike's reply doesn't refer to the FBI operation, which he now feels is relatively unimportant. Instead, Mike says to Connie, "I came here to tell your husband to keep his hands off my woman."

It's the good heart that distinguishes Angela and Mike from the rest of the film's characters. They live in the real world and embrace it with love and compassion. Not so for the gangster characters—they're off in fantasyville, which is perhaps why they don't react to the film's murders; the gang slayings are *all* examples of laser tag to them. Yet when the film shifts to Miami Beach, the audience enters a kind of fantasy land (albeit a visual one) too. The establishing shots of Miami show it to be a pastel-colored city built in praise of overt consumerism.

It's here that Tak Fujimoto's fluid camerawork comes into its own, the camera panning past the Eden Roc hotel just as the water shoots up out of its fountains, the editing and cinematography seamlessly functioning together when Tony has a vision in which he recalls all of Mike's various guises (and even one in which he doesn't appear: a beat officer's blue uniform, which definitely brands him as a cop). Tony's vision brings it all together for him: first the strangeness of Angela's agreeing to go with him to Miami, then the images that he sees in response to Mike, in tourist guise, walking past him in the lobby: Connie referring to "the schmuck Angela was shacked up with," the sight of the JD (probably for "Justice Department") plumber (a Watergate pun) whom Mike was posing as, as well as the airline captain whom Tony had seen the same day—all of them Mike "in disguise." Tony's insight clinches it, as does the bugged ring that Tony gets from Angela (Angela is already wearing the death necklace that Tony had given her). All that remains in the Miami scenes is the encounter and shootout in Tony's suite, which reveals Tony and Connie's antipathy and destructiveness and Mike and Angela's devotion (each of the latter risks their life to save the other).

Tony's final vision, his nightmare of Connie shooting off his genitals with a sawed-off shotgun—a very comic scene given the fact that Tony seems more afraid of Connie than of the grand jury—is more than a replay of the scene in the Miami hotel suite during which Tony, after saying he'd change, had seen Connie aim her gun at his groin. Tony's jailhouse dream, with Connie's gunshot sound blending in with the sound of prison doors slamming, makes it clear that Tony's greatest emasculation fear is imprisonment. Yet justice is finally done. The

Angela and Mike at the Federal Courts Building

law punishes the lawless (Tony) and frees the just (Mike and Angela) to pursue a romantic relationship.

At *Married to the Mob*'s end, Mike and Angela are finally reunited. Angela, now a full-fledged hairdresser in charge of her own life, has radically changed from our first view of her. She's no longer being molded into someone else's image of the proper woman; indeed, rather than being done over by a mob-associated hairdresser, she's now styling other people's hair. And in an extension of this reversal, Angela not only doesn't have her hair done by a man; she does a man's hair, in this case Mike's. She completely controls Mike, too, slamming his head back and forth over the sink, finally taking the sexual initiative by sitting on his lap. Then, complementing what Mike had said about her deserving a second chance, Angela brings the moral ellipsis to a close by giving Mike "another chance," which he's earned because of his willingness to risk himself for her, a demonstration that his journey toward enlightenment is complete. It's therefore appropriate that after the end titles, in footage that is integral to the film, we see Mike and Angela, after the dance party, emerging from the symbolic mist of uncertainty in which the film's mob-related events had plunged them, and gazing smilingly at the Federal Courts Building in downtown Manhattan, because it is by virtue of the federal legal system that Angela has been freed from the oppression of the mob and gained her new lover. Mike and Angela, though, make the location a lovers' playground, doing a charming dance on the courtroom steps. At the dance's end, in a whimsical inversion of the usual direction that Demme's sexual morality works, it's the woman who falls, and the man who saves her. We leave the couple in a frozen tableau, in the midst of redemption, saved from the end point of that fall, having been given that important second chance to live the good, upright life which they both want and cherish and which they'll now be able to have, with the added benefit that they'll finally be able to have it with each other.

10 | Screams

Demme was offered the chance to direct *The Silence of the Lambs* (1991) after Gene Hackman—for whom Orion had bought the Thomas Harris book—decided not to direct the film because of reservations he had about the story's violence. Demme also seems to have thought carefully before accepting the project, this despite his respect for Ted Tally, whom he knew had written the screenplay. "I was repelled by the idea of doing a film about a serial killer. Quite apart from do you want to make a film of it, do you want to see a film of it? [Then] I started reading the book, when Orion sent it to me, and I leapt at the chance to get involved with characters of such dimension, and a story with so many complicated and interesting themes."[1]

The rather grim story of a young FBI trainee, Clarice Starling (Jodie Foster), who—despite being discounted by every authority figure she meets, with the exception of the brilliant yet insane Dr. Hannibal Lecter (Anthony Hopkins)—nonetheless manages to find and stop serial killer Jame Gumb (Ted Levine), seems to have indicated treatment different from Demme's usual films. Gone are all the quirky little Demme touches. As Demme explains: "What was at the forefront was too important to be distracted by the details on the fringe."[2]

Even the roles given to Demme's friends and stock company are played straighter. Roger Corman appears as the director of the FBI; director George Romero appears in the courthouse scene. Scott Glenn (who was in both *Angels Hard as They Come* and *Fighting Mad*) plays FBI field director Jack Crawford, while Tracey Walter and Charles Napier respectively play a funeral home employee and a policeman.

Demme had learned from his failed efforts on *Last Embrace* what not to do in making a Hitchcock-like thriller. Also, with a budget of nineteen million dollars, he could afford to get the look he wanted. During post-production, Demme explained:

Now, though, I understand the Hitchcock style. I'm not trying to copy it; I'm using it in a fashion that I understand. I understand the style's strengths, I know when to employ it, and I've embraced it more and more in my own quiet way, not necessarily in terms of visual flamboyance but more in the use of subjective camera and how to photograph actors to communicate story and character points.[3]

Demme also employs the Hitchcock point-of-view shot. Since he wants the audience to identify with Clarice, hers are the views we usually get throughout the film. Yet in Clarice's confrontation with Gumb in his darkened basement, we see things from the killer's vantage point, through the infrared glasses. While Demme hoped that "perhaps the abandonment of Clarice's point of view will make the situation even more distressing on a certain dialectical level,"[4] it might also, had it been used earlier, have been a way for us to have understood Gumb, whose depersonalization (hence, our total alienation from him) in part prevents us from accepting that his dark nature exists inside of us also.

In set design, Demme tried to escape cliché. Demme says: "Kristi Zea—the production designer—and I spent a tremendous amount of time trying to deal with the bars on Lecter's cage. We were never happy with the different looks we were experimenting with. And finally we went to glass. The looks of Lecter's environments are sort of one step beyond, one step into active imagination in the presence of a lot of ultra realism elsewhere in the picture."[5]

Although *Silence of the Lambs* is the director's most commercially successful film, garnering five Academy Awards including Best Picture, Best Director, Best Actor, and Best Actress, it is in certain ways ethically problematical. While Demme's film version of the book preserves and amplifies the theme of Starling's resistance to being stereotyped and restricted by virtue of her femininity, it also spotlights Hannibal Lecter in such a way as to elevate him to a position of attractive prominence that, given Lecter's objectionable aspects, he simply doesn't deserve, and leaves Gumb open to being interpreted as a homosexual.

Silence of the Lambs is most strongly about affinities. Indeed, except for Clarice's pursuit of Gumb through his basement at the film's end (a duel-like interview of a sort), *Silence*'s major scenes all involve two-person interviews: those between Clarice and Jack Crawford, Clarice and Lecter's warder, Chilton (Anthony Heald), Clarice and Lecter, and Clarice and Gumb, with Clarice always on the end of at-

Clarice and one of her adversaries, Jame
Gumb

tempted manipulations by men. The film emphasizes the intensely
personal nature of these interactions, in particular the way that conversation is used to reveal the most intimate details of one's life. In this
film, unlike Demme's others, self-knowledge never effects any modifi-
cation in a character. In fact, none of *Silence*'s characters progresses in
any way, a radical change from the book, in which, after the rescue of
Catherine Martin, Clarice's formerly disturbed sleep is quite peaceful.
Contrast this situation with some of Demme's other films and you'll
see what a departure this is for the director. Through a confrontation
with darkness and death, *Something Wild*'s Charlie and Audrey and
Philadelphia's Andrew learn a great deal about themselves. Frank de
Marco's death gives *Married to the Mob*'s Angela a chance to escape
from mob domination and forge a new life for herself. Although the
ascendancy over death in *Silence* affords Clarice a way of proving her
mettle (she triumphs over Gumb), the experience does virtually nothing to advance her on a personal level. In fact, it's quite clear that in
contrast to all other central Demme characters, Clarice's emotional aspect is never made accessible to us, an issue to which we'll return.

All of *Silence of the Lambs*'s conversations center on sex and the use of language as determinants of social responsibility and status, and further reveal how strongly the film is concerned with investigating the manner in which women are manipulated: from the office politics employed by Crawford, to Chilton's sexual invitation, to the personality probing by Lecter, and finally to the insidious toying (but with a murderous intent) by Gumb. The irony in the film, which we will discuss further, is that of all of these manipulative men, it is Hannibal Lecter, the most accomplished killer among them (all of the men in one sense or another attempt to murder Clarice, by trying to either kill her or destroy the integrity of her personality), who in some ways treats Clarice with the most gentleness and respect, and who is the only one among them who to a degree is really interested in her as a person, not as an object to be manipulated. This fact may explain why Lecter is the only character allowed to have intimate physical contact with Clarice, in the finger touch (an obvious corollary of the God and Adam finger gesture from Michelangelo's Sistine Chapel fresco) that is, paradoxically, at once a gesture of friendship and an obvious corollary for intercourse.

Clarice is the film's center, and is often the recipient of attentions that she either doesn't solicit (as with Pilcher) or even want (as is the case with Chilton). But as Lecter so cunningly realizes, what Clarice is really searching for is a lost male parent. Like *Star Wars*' Luke Skywalker, she finds one in the person of a dark father (which is one way of reading the name of the *Star Wars* character Darth Vader), in this case Hannibal Lecter, who, given the film's emphasis on sex, is at once father and lover, at once distant (in the role of therapist, even though he performs "therapy" on Clarice for his pleasure) and involved (in the role of someone who has affection for Clarice). It is appropriate, too, that for Clarice, who throughout the film seems destined to be a loner, her father/lover should once again recede into unreachability at the film's end. Thus, at *Silence*'s conclusion, Clarice and Lecter can only communicate by voice. As with her real father, it is murder that separates Clarice and Lecter, with only two of Lecter's fingers lingering for a moment over the phone after he has hung up on Clarice, thus breaking their contact forever.

It is characteristic of Demme that he should have stressed the female element in *Silence of the Lambs*, since it isn't just a film about women being abducted and killed but is also about women being either manipulated or murdered in ways that are analogues of the sanctioned types of violence (which we've seen through the actions of characters like *Something Wild*'s Ray and *Married to the Mob*'s Tony) indigenous to American culture.

The comparisons between elements in American culture and Gumb's murderous behavior, whose victimizing effects are apparent, start off seeming obvious enough. Clarice is a small woman. At the film's beginning she gets onto an elevator with men who are much taller than she is.[6] While running on the FBI track, Clarice and her friend Ardelia (Kasi Lemmons) are covertly ogled by male trainees. A tall man (identified as "Airport Flirt" in the credits) intentionally crosses in front of Clarice just so that he can get a good look at her. When considered along with more insidious instances of Clarice being singled out because of her size and sex, these examples of harassment, many of which *Silence*'s audiences respond to with the laughter of recognition, show how self-conscious Clarice is always made to feel.

Even if they've read about the effects of racial or sexual bias, many white American males have never experienced it, have no idea what it feels like to be discriminated against merely because of your appearance.[7] If you are a woman, the world is full of threats against you by men, which begin with unwelcome provocative glances or intentional double entendres and work all the way up to murder. It is therefore highly ironic that the film's main perpetrator of violence against women, Jame Gumb, wants to become a woman, not only in behavior (which he apes twice, once when Catherine Martin is screaming, the other time when he is dancing alone, at that point replete with makeup and wig), but in actual physical characteristics as well. As Gumb says to an imaginary man during his solo dance scene, "Would you fuck me; I'd fuck me," even going so far as to tuck his penis between his legs to mimic the appearance of female genitalia.

Much of the film has to do with things sensory, moving from eye contacts (thus the strong emphasis on close-ups); to sounds (for example, the creaks and groans in the asylum and in Gumb's basement at *Silence*'s end, or the noise of the expelled air that emerges from the funeral parlor corpse of one of Gumb's victims after a cocoon is extracted from her throat);[8] to smells (Clarice's perfume and the stench from the bloated corpse of one of Gumb's victims). This emphasis on sensory stimuli makes it all the more apparent that the interplay between Clarice and Lecter, while of a highly intellectual nature, is not only a substitute for sensory contact between them, but also pushes Clarice up against memories that are highly sensual in nature (this is the substance of Lecter's "therapy" on Clarice).

If "memory . . . is what [Lecter has] instead of a view" (there's the implicit suggestion that part of the meaning of Lecter's restricted view is figurative, involving a severed moral sensibility), Lecter also uses his views into Clarice's memories to restore to him access to the world outside of his jail cell. Indeed, during their interviews, Lecter lives through Clarice's memories: the painfully recalled death of her father, the sounds of the screaming lambs, the feel of the cold air when she flees her cousin's sheep and horse ranch.

In essence, Lecter's compelling Clarice to remember does more than vicariously serve up to him the delectable sensations that Clarice experienced when the events on which her memories are based actually took place. (Like predatory rapists and murderers, Lecter enjoys others' pain, drinking it in; the policeman in Baltimore isn't far from wrong when he asks Clarice if Lecter isn't "some kind of vampire," a walking dead feeding off of the living.) It also brings Clarice closer to that final reconciliation with the past and the loss of her father that she needs in order to properly qualify as an agent of a police force that at all times requires her to operate at the peak of efficiency.

We do not get the sense in the film, as we do in Thomas Harris's book,[9] that Lecter is able to withdraw within himself into silence and stoicism. The film's Lecter seems starved for attention; he becomes quite dependent upon Clarice's visits. Thus, when Lecter is stung by Clarice's false offer of a change in his place of confinement, he bitterly expresses his anger and disappointment in terms of affection. "People will say we're in love," Lecter sarcastically says, but in an important sense, he means this statement sincerely; he truly admires Clarice for her impressive amount of self-knowledge. "You're very frank," Lecter earlier tells Clarice. "I think it would be quite something to know you in private life."

Lecter is only granted access to Clarice publicly, yet he forces her to reveal to him her innermost thoughts and feelings, thereby establishing an intimate bond between them. And though Lecter tells Clarice nothing revelatory about himself (a clear example of his maintaining the predominant position in their relationship), he implicitly expresses to her through his incisive and probing manner, and his powerful desire for her reactions, how much he needs interaction with a woman like Clarice, who can match him alternation for alternation between business-like coolness and passionate expression. (How else, other than as an example of creation that gives pleasure to the creator, are we to understand the joy that Lecter doubtless takes in his escape and the way in which he arranges the escape scene for the express titillation of the policemen who find Boyle's disemboweled corpse?)

There is a rather objectionable class issue in the film, one that works against Demme's usual populism. Lecter tells Clarice that she is "only one generation away from poor white trash." In this scene it appears as though Demme is critical of Lecter's class-abusive references; yet despite the sensitive portrayal of Belvedere, Ohio, and Clarice's home town, the film condemns the lower classes by directing our sympathies toward Lecter and against Gumb. After all, what real difference is there between Lecter and Gumb aside from the fact that Lecter is well-read and well-spoken, while Gumb is barely able to fumble out two coherent sentences? Although it's clear that Lecter and Gumb are strong counterparts, not only in that they are both serial killers but also in that they like to put on masks—Gumb in the form of the woman's guise that he assumes, Lecter by either appropriating different dialects or, during his escape, using the fleshy mask of officer Pembry, which he finally discards in favor of the wig and sunglasses he's wearing at the film's end—*Silence of the Lambs* nonetheless goes out of its way to condemn Gumb and glorify Lecter, an example of the film's haphazard morality.

Yet this bias toward white, educated, accomplished males manifests itself at other points in the film as well: in what is meant to be an amusing comment by Pilcher (Paul Lazar) that his colleague's statements should be ignored because "he's not a Ph.D." (an assertion that links up with Lecter's reference to Clarice's only being a "trainee"), and in the poor location afforded Gumb's house, which is mirrored in the small-town poverty of the Bimmel home (which, like Gumb's, is close to a set of railroad tracks). Demme is at his best in characterizing the Bimmel neighborhood, giving us shots of a whirligig turning in a slow, melancholy fashion; of a bird house; of a bored-looking woman gazing out of a second story window,[10] and tries to show us the homey quality of a similar neighborhood, the town in which Clarice grew up, where everyone seems to know everyone else's name. Yet one can't escape the feeling that, as in *Married to the Mob*, whose hero remains an FBI man at the film's end, Demme is ambivalently attracted to the law enforcement power structure, prominent among whose objectionable values is a bias against the lower classes.[11]

Given the book's potential for excess, Demme and screenwriter Ted Tally have done a remarkable job of toning down its more exploitative aspects. Tally has trimmed away the parts of the book that he and Demme apparently felt deviated from its central theme: Clarice's search in a male-dominated world for a confirmation of her strength and will power. Unfortunately, at the same time they have lost a great many character touches that personalized the novel, among them the story of Crawford's dying wife, the deletion of which effectively denies Crawford any shred of compassion, since now all that we see is his business side. We may hear Crawford express concern for Clarice, but at these points his emotion seems unconvincing. And while the film certainly succeeds in making Lecter a fascinating character, this is no great accomplishment; Lecter was just as intriguing in the book.

As in the case of Crawford, Gumb receives short shrift in terms of insightful characterization; like *Something Wild*'s Ray, he's given no background (as he is, albeit sketchily, in the novel, where we learn that he spent his early life in various institutions, first as an orphan and then as a young murderer), so that he seems to be more a character type than a character. During the scene in which Gumb is dancing in his basement (one of the most effective sequences in the entire film), there is only the barest suggestion that Gumb's pathological nature partially derives from his isolation and his fierce desire to have someone love him. Yet since the scene's suggested meanings are never developed, we tend to concentrate far more on the excessive action, which panders to the more outlandish aspects of Gumb's character: his makeup, his use of a nipple clip (the sight of which always elicits cries of dismay from the audience, as though Gumb's wearing this harmless object somehow summed up everything that is wrong with him), and his simulation of female genitalia.

One of the book's most interesting themes, the question of responsibility, is passed over by the film. In the book, Clarice tells Lecter that, perhaps, he should be curious "about why you're here [in the asylum]. About what happened to you." Lecter replies,

> Nothing happened to me, Officer Starling. *I* happened. You can't reduce me to a set of influences. You've given up good and evil for behaviorism, Officer Starling. You've got everybody in moral dignity pants—nothing is ever anybody's fault. Look at me, Officer Starling. Can you stand to say I'm evil? Am I evil, Officer Starling?[12]

Clarice's reply is somewhat inconclusive. "I think you've been destructive. For me, it's the same thing," she says. But as Lecter points out, "then *storms* are evil, if it's that simple."[13] The book's Lecter is advocating accountability for himself and, by implication, Gumb—this despite Gumb's background as a neglected child. In contrast, the closest the film's Lecter comes to this sort of discussion is when he suggests that while searching for Buffalo Bill (the name that a local police department has given the killer), Starling look at suspects who were abused in the past; Lecter seems to be taking the behaviorist side in the issue here, the opposite of his viewpoint in the book. While it might have been difficult for the film to dramatize the two sides in this debate, a reference to the distinction between behaviorism and personal responsibility, or, preferably, the inclusion of some of this issue's discussion from the book, would have added an intellectual dimension that might have significantly improved our understanding of Lecter and Gumb's personalities.

But then no character seems to have a background except Clarice. After losing her biological father at an early age, she encounters two father figures in the film, one (Crawford) supposedly representing truth and light, the other (Lecter) a grim figure. The irony is that it's Crawford who reinforces Clarice's position as an underling condemned to servitude as a sexual inferior, whereas it's Lecter, the maligned, dark figure, who reminds Clarice of the oppressive pain that she feels over her father's death. Lecter carries out these actions for two distinct and opposed motives: because he likes to manipulate people (after all, Lecter repeatedly withholds from Clarice his information about Gumb), and because he has genuine affection and respect for Clarice, and wants her to confront the most traumatic event in her life in order to pass beyond the pain that it continues to cause her. Unfortunately, with the departure of Lecter, Clarice is thrown back for moral support on the FBI, which acts as her family, yet which is hardly a family that recommends itself given the bureau's authoritarian attitude and sexual biases. (There's a hint, though, that with the graduation of Clarice and Ardelia, a new FBI, tempered with a more accepting, female-influenced perspective, may be in the offing).

Some people might object that since Gumb is a murderer, he doesn't deserve our sympathy. How then can we explain audiences' fascination with another murderer, Lecter, a reaction evident to anyone who has seen the film theatrically? It's these same people who are cheering Lecter on at the film's end as he goes off in pursuit of Chilton. The film evidences an elitist attitude and a moral dualism. For all of *Silence*'s well-intentioned references to sexual discrimination, this issue seems more peripheral than central. Demme tries to keep this concern at the film's center but he can't; the action involving Lecter and the abductions by Gumb is too engrossing. Of course, the book and film are concerned with Clarice's triumph over adversarial conditions, but predominantly, both works also pander to the baser instincts involved with giving the audience thrills. As Lecter would say, the film's dramatization of issues involving sexual discrimination is "incidental. What does [it] do, this [film that you're discussing]?" The answer seems to be that it intends to provide jolts of excitement.

Demme tries to be both tasteful and realistic; he wants to communicate the truth about murder and its gruesome aspects without descending into exploitation, and for the most part he achieves this goal. The film's use of photography (for example, the way that an ominous atmosphere is created even in brightly lit scenes) is impressive. But the production lacks the characteristic Demme wit, a grievous oversight in a film whose depressing subject matter cries out for a little relief. Moreover, by failing to present us with an empathetic base for his film, Demme has left us, like Clarice in Gumb's basement, groping around in the dark. We can respect Demme's attempt to deal with important ideas here; in how many other films has the issue of serial killing received so much intelligent attention? But Demme seems to have approached his subject matter too seriously. In *Silence* he's lost the distance from his film that would have allowed him to realize that although there are inhuman aspects to the subject matter, we still need to see recognizably human characters dealing with the action's problematical aspects. Failing this, what we're left with is more of a clinical study than a drama.

Many of the film's scenes incorporate symbolic camera movements (the restless tracking shots in Gumb's basement mirror our concern with what is going on there) and fascinating dialogue (the discussions between Clarice and Lecter show each character alternating between emotional involvement—Lecter is interested in Clarice's past, Clarice is reliving painful memories—and clinical detachment, characterized by Lecter's cool approach to Clarice's revelations and Clarice's professional interest in obtaining information about Buffalo Bill). Also noteworthy is Demme's use of actor placement and gestures: Lecter and Clarice on opposite sides of the plastic shield, Lecter turning away when Clarice talks about her private life as though he were a priest hearing someone's confession, with the shield acting as the confessional screen, one of the many symbolic barriers between them that is absent during the latter part of their fourth, most intimate interview, when Demme zooms in on their faces so closely that the metal bars of the cage in which Lecter is now contained can no longer be seen. The funeral home sequence during which Clarice, in her imagination, drifts into the service to stare down into the coffin where, through a memory projection from the past, her father is lying, is a triumph of sensitive technique.

The film gives us plenty of details to ponder, from Clarice's slight stature (which is at odds with her impressive self-command) to the quote from the e. e. cummings poem "buffalo bill's" ("how do you like your blue-eyed boy / mister death?") on the blackboard of an office into which Clarice stops to inquire about Crawford. Ostensibly referring to the couch with which he is struggling, Gumb tells Catherine

Martin that he's having trouble "get[ting] it up in the truck." When she helps him, he tells her to "push it all the way up," both obvious sexual references. These and similar statements mark *Silence of the Lambs* as the most literary of Demme's films, a quality doubtless accruing from Ted Tally's screenplay. But this aspect isn't necessarily a virtue. The meanings of Demme's films don't usually inhere in individual references so much as in the films' emotional feel, in our admiration for the way that the characters get themselves into and out of trouble as they grope toward a better life. The fact that *Silence of the Lambs* is often reducible to particulars makes it in some ways less interesting than Demme's other films.

As in *Caged Heat*, what Demme is once again trying to do is blend two very different genres, exploitation and social critique. Regardless of the honesty of the attempt, he hasn't quite succeeded. This is not so say that *Silence* is not well crafted or constructed. The discussions between Clarice and Crawford are a case in point. In all of his talks with Clarice, Crawford is careful to maintain a degree of distance. Although the initial scene between Crawford and Clarice seems merely expository, it is in fact comprised of a series of statements whose rhetoric establishes the prescribed place that each of the characters is to occupy. The discussion is also the first of the interviews involving Clarice, establishing a pattern of question and response that will be repeated throughout the film.

Careful to make sure that Clarice remembers she is no more than a student, and therefore an inferior, Crawford first greets her as though he is calling the role of a class. "Starling, Clarice M.," he says when he first enters his office. Crawford tells Clarice that her instructors say she is doing well; Clarice answers with what we will come to recognize as her usual degree of humility and restraint. "I hope so; they haven't posted any grades yet," she says. In a similar display of professional control, Clarice refuses to be emotionally drawn into reacting to taunting remarks offered by Lecter. Unlike Senator Martin, who is hurt by Lecter's comment about her nursing her daughter, Clarice doesn't allow Lecter to get an emotional rise out of her. When Lecter asks Clarice if she thinks that Crawford desires her sexually, Clarice tells Lecter that she never thinks about it.

For Crawford, it's important that he keep reminding Clarice of her subsidiary role; Crawford's compulsion reveals his insecurity with regard to his own position. Crawford says, "A job's come up—not a job, really, more of an interesting errand." Clarice is thus an errand person, nothing more. "The one [serial killer] we want [to interview] most [Lecter] refuses to cooperate. I want you to go after him again today,"

Chilton taunting Lecter

says Crawford, making it clear from his use of the word "again" that previous agents have failed in their efforts to get Lecter to talk. Apparently, Crawford sends Clarice to the asylum for the reason that Chilton divines: because she's young and attractive, precisely (in Chilton's words) "[Lecter's] taste." Yet when Clarice suspects a link between the assignment and the Buffalo Bill killings, Crawford abruptly cuts her off with a remark that tells Clarice in no uncertain terms that it's none of her business, and that he considers such inquiries out of her realm. "Excuse me, sir, but why the urgency? . . . Is there some connection between [Lecter] and Buffalo Bill?" Clarice asks, to which Crawford replies, "I wish there were. Now I want your full attention, Starling," the derogatory use of the last name indicating that Crawford is telling Clarice to stay in her place.

The fact is that Crawford doesn't respect Clarice's abilities, now or later in the film. When Clarice later complains to Crawford that she just wishes she'd been "in on it" (the full details of her assignment), Crawford replies, "If I had sent you in there with an actual agenda, Lecter would have known it instantly. He would have toyed with you, then turned to stone." Yet Crawford is obviously wrong. When Clarice does go to Lecter with an "actual agenda," the false Plum Island offer, Lecter doesn't realize that it's a ruse until Chilton tells him so.

Like Crawford, Chilton also dehumanizes people. He refers to

Lecter checking Clarice's "identification"

Lecter as "our most prized asset" and reduces Clarice to a sexual object by propositioning her. When he is turned down, he becomes viciously clinical. Also like Crawford, Chilton starts to rattle off a series of regulations. Crawford told Clarice to follow the asylum's procedures partially as a way of keeping her in line; Chilton reinforces this attitude by outlining these procedures, which he does after insulting Clarice's educational background (Clarice: "I graduated from UVa, Doctor. It's not a charm school." Chilton: "Good. Then you should be able to remember the rules").

The buildup to the first interview between Clarice and Lecter is slow and intense. Chilton takes Clarice into the asylum's bowels, into Hell if we are to judge not only by the depths to which they descend but also by the garish red light that suffuses the two characters when Chilton shows Clarice the picture of the nurse whom Lecter attacked. Demme overloads the soundtrack with groans and deep noises (Skip Lievsay's sound work is very expressive here), but he dissipates all of our tension when we first see Lecter, who initially seems harmless enough. Essentially, the discussions between Clarice and Lecter pun on the word "identity," one of Demme's perennial concerns. Clarice is trying to discover Buffalo Bill's identity, his name. Lecter, though, isn't concerned with such a superficial approach to a person's individuality; he wants to know things about people's psychologies. Clarice identifies herself by name; Lecter asks to see her identification. When Clarice brings the identification card close to the glass of Lecter's cell, though, what Lecter initially looks at isn't the card but Clarice's eyes. He's not interested in her public identity, then, but in her deeper self. Yet before he will talk to her, Lecter has to decide if she is worth the time it will take to know her. He therefore tests Clarice. Using a technique of which Crawford and Chilton would approve, Lecter insults Clarice. "That [card] expires in one week. You're not real FBI, are you?" Lecter asks. Clarice replies forthrightly, with a deftness of rhetoric that impresses Lecter. "I'm a student; I'm here to learn from you. Maybe you can decide for yourself whether or not I'm qualified enough to do that," Clarice says. Lecter is cognizant of the double bind in which Clarice's statement places him. Only two possible responses to her assertion are possible: either Lecter accepts Clarice as legitimate, so that there is no discussion of her qualifications, or, if he should consider her a priori unqualified, he needs to talk to her to decide whether or not his intuition is correct. No matter how he answers, then, if he responds to the question as worded, Lecter must continue to talk to Clarice. "Hmm," Lecter says, "That's rather slippery of you." But Clarice has clearly earned Lecter's respect (which is also gained as a result of her forthrightly repeating Miggs's assertion, "I can smell your cunt"), because Lecter finishes the statement by calling her "*Agent* Starling" (emphasis added; the reference contrasts with Lecter's previous outrage over Jack Crawford's having "sent a *trainee* to me") and politely inviting her to sit down.

Although Lecter objects to what he refers to as Clarice's "ham-handed segue into [her] questionnaire" (she puns on the word "view"), Lecter shouldn't really protest, since he performs a "ham-handed segue," punning on the word "terns/turns" during their third meeting. It's the idea that Clarice is acting as Crawford's surrogate, using the questionnaire as an excuse to get information out of him, that infuriates Lecter. But when, during their second meeting, Clarice passes the test of decoding his anagram about Miss Mofet, Lecter not only acts compassionately toward Clarice by offering her a towel for her wet hair but also decides to talk to her again. Disarmed by her candor and intuition, and only half playing with her, teasing her with his information about Buffalo Bill, Lecter slowly leads Clarice to the killer. At no time, though, does Lecter ever tell Clarice anything about himself. He refuses, in Clarice's words, to "turn [his] high-powered perception" on himself. Throughout the film, Clarice and Lecter's discussions act as another example of one-sided sexual relationships; although Lecter calls her Clarice, Clarice never calls Lecter anything other than "doctor," a formality that always works in Lecter's favor.[14]

By the time of their fourth interview, in the Memphis courthouse,

Lecter—although at first angry with Clarice—will draw out of Clarice her second-most-important memory: her attempt to rescue a spring lamb that is scheduled for slaughter. The fact that the rescue fails, that the lamb is killed, and that her cousin's husband is so angry that he sends her to a state home means that, as with the death of her father, Clarice is not only once more deprived of a father figure, but is once again orphaned, thus learning for the second time what it means to be cast into an emotional darkness. This quality, combined with Clarice's realization (under Lecter's prompting) that she equates the sacrificial lambs with Gumb's victims, and that, by her own admission, she often wakes up at night hearing (in Lecter's words) "the awful screaming of the lambs," indicates that she is uniquely qualified as the precise person to identify with the women whom Gumb abducts, all of whom find themselves separated from their families and cast into a perilous gloom.[15]

It may seem throughout the film that Clarice is quite well adjusted, that she has learned how to deal with the routine insults and dilemmas that life poses for her. How, then, are we to understand the severe trauma that she often relives, which would still be powerfully suppressed had it not been for Lecter's perverse ministrations? Is Clarice in the FBI because of a kind of overcompensation, a need to make up for the loss of her father by replacing him with the bureau? There's no way to tell. What we do know is that after she breaks down crying in the asylum parking lot after Lecter's initial reference to her father, Clarice is next seen on the FBI artillery range, firing a hand gun with fierce determination. Through the juxtaposition of the scenes, Demme seems to be telling us that there are two realms in which Clarice operates: that of the vulnerable woman, and that of the FBI agent—and, further, that it doesn't seem as though for Clarice there is any middle ground between these realms.

The film only gives us a slight glimpse of a Clarice who seems relaxed and accessible: when, in her own words, Pilcher is "hitting on" her. However, Clarice's choice of words to describe Pilcher's behavior is quite severe. Pilcher's question to her—"Ever go out for cheeseburgers and beer . . . the amusing house wine?"—seems more like an innocent request for a date than a sexual proposition, which is how we understand the term "hitting on." Demme either distracts us from considering the way that Clarice's personality is severely bifurcated, or else he is representing to us what he views as the "correct" personality for women. We suspect that what we are seeing in *Silence of the Lambs* is an exaggeration of assertive female characteristics, melded with the psyche of a law enforcement officer. The same type of psychological makeup as Clarice's is present in *Married to the Mob*'s Mike Downey. The essential difference is that *Married* had Mike exhibit accessibility and personal quirkiness, characteristics that a woman on a case like Clarice's can't afford. (In this respect, Demme may have been wrong in casting Jodie Foster in the film, since she seems incapable of giving a hint that Clarice is anything other than a hard-as-steel personality).

It's easy to see why *Silence of the Lambs* was so extraordinarily popular: the film is witty and thrilling. Nevertheless, we can't help feeling that in this film, Demme has to a degree obscured some of his more attractive directorial qualities. *Silence* is virtually humorless when it should be wry, insensitive to the way that it manipulates characters (even those characters, like Gumb, who are villainous), and incognizant of the manner in which it implicitly lends approbation both to a sexually and socially repressive regime like the FBI and to the character of Hannibal Lecter, who for all of his charm is nonetheless a serial killer. At the film's end, that "roar [of] approval" (to use Demme's words)[16] when the audience realizes that Lecter intends to kill Chilton may signal a bonanza at the box office, but it also highlights a certain compromise on the part of its director, who, in an apparent repudiation of his ethical ellipsis (only Chilton reaps the rewards of his negative karma for abusing Lecter, but no such retribution seems slated for Lecter), is here endorsing murder. Judging by the director's next film—*Philadelphia*, a story about an AIDS-infected lawyer who protests his firm's firing him—it's a mistake in morals that Demme will not allow himself to repeat.

11 | Love and Death

For a follow-up film to *The Silence of the Lambs*, an occasionally excessive thriller, *Philadelphia* (1993) is remarkably tame. The first high-profile Hollywood movie to deal with AIDS and its impact on an individual, the film generated an appreciable amount of press. The majority of the positive responses to *Philadelphia*, though, were surprisingly mediocre in their enthusiasm,[1] while the most prominent negative review (by *The Nation*'s Stuart Klawans)[2] severely denigrated the film for its middle-of-the-road approach to AIDS, when what Klawans obviously would have preferred was more direct dealing with the issue of the disease, more depiction of gay lifestyle, and less restraint in characterizing the relationship between Andy Beckett (Tom Hanks, in an Academy Award-winning performance) and his lover Miguel (Antonio Banderas). Moreover, critics of the film seized on the character of lawyer Joe Miller (Denzel Washington) as being too much of a representative type, a straight black male whose situation on the one hand so obviously contrasts with that of Andy, and yet whose status as a potential outsider supposedly gives him some affinity with the man who eventually becomes his client. This easy fit between Andy and Joe led some critics to claim that the film was guilty of forcing social issues in a blatant fashion; indeed, Klawans referred to Demme as having unwittingly transformed himself into Stanley Kramer.[3]

After asserting incorrectly that the outcome of the film's trial is never shown, *Newsweek* complained of the "truncated view of [the] hero's personal life," going on to state that the film "has the feel of a movie made from the outside in."[4] *Time*'s Richard Corliss wrote that Andy's law firm cooked up "a phony excuse to fire him" (although this point is never established in the film), and talked about how the film, as with others on Holocaust-like subjects, instead of building scenes "deftly, allusively," "accumulate[s] horrific detail to make sure you get the point,"[5] a criticism that surely doesn't apply to *Philadel-*

phia, whose "horrific detail[s]" are virtually nonexistent. Additionally, the film does not imply, as Corliss would have you believe, that "the death threat hanging over gays commands our sympathy for them,"[6] but merely expects that a sensitive audience will be able to identify with its central character. And though, as we'll see, there is a reason for the pronounced acceptance on the part of Andy's family, it's simply not fair of some critics to characterize the family's responses as unreal, nor to depict their counterparts, the members of Andy's law firm, as "crumb-buns."[7] Only when Corliss states with regard to certain aspects of the film that "nothing in the real world is quite as simple as this"[8] does he, albeit inadvertently, provide us with a successful way of approaching this deceptively simple film.

Many of these criticisms seem to emanate from misunderstandings and misrepresentations that seem virtually willful. A more productive approach would have been to attempt to place the film in the context of Demme's other work, within which it would emerge as an example of romantic stylization. Additionally, many critics seem to have approached Andy's character from an intellectual rather than an emotional viewpoint. This is not to say that such critics' objections are not correct if for them the characters ring false. But as we've stressed throughout this book, the ultimate success of Demme's films derives from the truth of the feelings being represented. At least in this respect, *Philadelphia* is as valid as any film that Demme has ever made.

Moreover, audiences are missing the point if they cannot somehow sympathize with Andy, who, having been diagnosed with AIDS, is from the film's beginning reacting to pressures and constraints that simply don't obtain for any other major character in the film. Being told that you have a terminal disease occasions a variety of emotional and physical responses: panic, denial, depression, and, perhaps most strikingly, an inability on the part of the rational consciousness to resign one's self to what is happening: the experiencing of a physical debility that drags down the mind and body with it, the realization that, to quote Yeats, one is "fastened to a dying animal, it knows not what it is . . ."[9] In the words of the Bruce Springsteen song that opens the film,[10] you become "unrecognizable to [your] self," "wast[e] away," hear the "voices of friends vanished and gone," and perceive one horrible day that your "clothes don't fit [you] no more"—in other words, the self experiences the loss of self, since death strikes its most telling blow against the identity. Corollary issues like these lend significance to *Philadelphia*; and while, as we'll see, the film commits certain errors of fact and logic in the courtroom scenes, it always seems

Philadelphia's Andy Beckett and Charles Wheeler

genuine and sincere, qualities that a purely cerebral reaction to the film cannot negate.

One might have expected easy characterizations from the film, but one doesn't get them. Despite the fact that Andy works for a large Philadelphia law firm, Wyant, Wheeler et al., and is first seen defending a moneyed client (the owners of a construction company), he later gladly embraces the cause of a company, Highline Inc., whose spreadsheet program has been stolen by a larger competitor. Although we are led to assume that Charles Wheeler (Jason Robards), one of the senior partners of Andy's firm, is warning Andy about which side in the case to choose when he refers to his friendship with the larger company's CEO, Wheeler is, in fact, delighted when Andy shows a preference for Highline's position. And while one might argue that, as with Microsoft, Highline, characterized as "an energetic young company," promises to become a big corporate abuser of its own, Wheeler seems to be encouraging Andy to choose sides based on idealistic legal merits, not practical ones.

From virtually the film's beginning, Andy acts as though his disease doesn't have important consequences. He rushes from the construction company argument in a judge's chambers to his appointment for an AZT treatment. While a fellow patient is telling a story about a waitress in a restaurant offering him Sweet n' Low instead of sugar, Andy glances over at another AIDS patient covered with Kaposi's Sarcoma sores, the veins in whose arms have collapsed, then returns to his headphone music and notetaking. Perhaps what we're seeing here is an example of Andy attempting to shut out the disease's grim realities. In any case, Andy has chosen to conceal his disease from others, doing so not only in conversation but in action as when, talking to one of the firm's senior partners, Walter Kenton (Robert Ridgely), Andy represents a KS lesion on his forehead as a bruise from a racquetball game. As in many other Demme films, what we see in *Philadelphia* is a character at the film's beginning disguising himself for the sake of survival in a world that to some extent is alien to him. Unlike *Something Wild*'s Audrey, Andy isn't trying on a different identity; he's more like *Married to the Mob*'s Angela, who at her film's beginning dissembles in order to survive. Each character, though, begins his or her proper assertion of self after repudiating this mode of deceit. In directly making known his gay nature, Andy begins to confront his impending death. Yet once he experiences the disease's full impact— first when he is compelled to go to a hospital emergency room, and, more forcefully, some time later after he has been fired and has lost much of his hair, two very direct blows to his already weakened sense of integrity—Andy, after unsuccessfully trying to get Joe Miller to represent him in a wrongful dismissal suit against the firm, is depicted as virtually falling apart. In a wonderful shot outside of Miller's office after Miller has refused to take Andy's case (Miller does so for personal reasons: his aversion to both AIDS and homosexuals),[11] Andy stands near the building, the facade of his identity shattered, at this point unable to fight back and regain some of his integrity by means of either personal or legal action. Motionless, Andy shifts his eyes back and forth and slowly panics, is only barely able to prevent himself from crying. Demme doesn't linger on the scene, merely holding Hanks in the frame long enough for us to gauge the effect of the feelings that his character is experiencing, and modifies the scene's effect by having passersby repeatedly walk between the camera and Andy, at once reminding us of the swirl of life that indifferently continues despite Andy's dilemma and tempering the shot's effect by periodically interrupting our views of Andy so that it doesn't seem as though the image is being forced on us.

The scene in the law library (which, judging from Andy's deteriorating condition, occurs weeks later) shows us Andy nursing a cold and being subjected to blatant discrimination because of his disease. Coincidentally, Joe is working at a desk a few feet away; in one interesting shot, a man slowly walks past Joe's table, all the while staring at him for what seems like a protracted amount of time. Whether the man is unaware of what he's doing or is attempting some sort of homosexual pick-up can't be determined; as in the scene outside of Joe's office, we're presented with a piece of dramatic action without directorial commentary, a testament to Demme's tendency to let actions, especially emotionally complex ones, speak for themselves.

The law librarian wants Andy to go to a private study carrel but Andy refuses. When Joe, after watching the scene from behind a stack of law books, comes over to Andy's table, there's a brief but interesting interplay among the three characters, in particular with regard to their eye movements, that represents additional evidence of Demme's ability to make small gestures meaningful. The law librarian, after hearing Andy's refusal to leave the area, still stands over Andy, while Andy, knowing that the man is there but unwilling to legitimize his presence by meeting his gaze, stares straight ahead, only looking at the man after he's asked if he'd be more comfortable in a separate section, and saying to him in a direct challenge to his hypocritical request, "No, would it make *you* more comfortable?" A stalemate has been reached that is broken by Joe's coming over to the table, first looking at Andy and then, catching the eyes of the law librarian, making it plain by the directness and effrontery of his look that he's already allied himself with Andy against this man's blatant manipulations, challenging the librarian to leave Andy alone, which he finally does after uttering the words "Whatever, sir," thus indicating that at least in his estimation, the encounter has ended equivocally.

Despite Joe's action, it's clear even after he discovers that Andy still doesn't have a lawyer that he hasn't decided to take Andy's case. However, Joe starts to become intrigued, first because his interest has been piqued by the two forms of discrimination (one apparent, one definite) that he's just seen—those involving, first, the man who stared at him, then the interplay between Andy and the librarian. However, Joe doesn't make up his mind until he finds out that Andy has discovered a legal precedent for his suit against Wyant, Wheeler, the Federal Vocational Rehabilitation Act of 1973, which, according to a text that Andy finds, led to subsequent decisions affirming that "AIDS is protected as a handicap under law" and that "the prejudice surrounding AIDS exacts a social death which precedes the actual physical one." When reading the latter passage, Andy falters on the word "precedes"; his hesitation, indicating that he is still terrified of dying, acts as a tasteful reminder of his situation.[12]

Although the legal judgment makes it clear that acting biased toward people with AIDS represents "the essence of discrimination," this point, and its possible relation to Joe's status as a black man, is never made an issue in the film. The only time that Joe is clearly singled out as a special case is when he is propositioned in a drugstore by a gay law student. Aside from the scene's improbability—it's doubtful that anyone who is gay would mistake Joe's sexual orientation—the scene works less as an attempt to establish an affinity between Joe and Andy's characters than as a reminder that despite his representing Andy, Joe's feelings about homosexuals haven't changed (he becomes outraged and physically abusive). Indeed, it's precisely in the film's refusal to dramatize in any way Joe's drawing a connection between his being black and Andy's being gay that points up its hands-off approach to characterization and, with the exception of the periodically awkward trial sequences, its insistence that the audience draw its own conclusions. As for Joe, the fact that the drugstore scene has no effect on his personal attitudes is made plain in a subsequent scene in a bar, in which he states that he still hates gays, but that the point in Andy's case is that a law has been broken, a consideration that takes precedence over one's personal opinions. Yet this pronouncement isn't allowed to be the film's final say on the matter of whether ideals should prevail. Thus later, although the trial judge points out that in his courtroom, justice is blind to matters of race, creed, and sexual preference, Joe points out that people don't live in the courtroom; they live in the real world, a further reminder of the film's awareness that there is a reprehensible and regrettable split between the realms of the real and the ideal.

As noted, some critics have objected that the scene with Andy's family, all of whom are strongly supportive of his court case and lifestyle, begs credibility. There's a priestly resignation and love being acted out here, a quality that Demme apparently meant to accentuate by having an actual minister, his cousin Robert Castle, play Andy's father. Yet what we're seeing in the family's actions is less an actual truth than an emotional one, a representation of the kind of affectionate, supportive family that all of us would like to have. The giddy sense of unreality that the scene invokes, with Andy somewhat unabashedly saying, "Gee, I love you guys," seems to represent Demme's innocent desire to see the ideal for a moment become real.

Especially as measured by Demme's standards, though, *Philadelphia* is somewhat disappointing. Demme has always taken pride in the fact that his films play well. However, it's difficult to avoid feeling that *Philadelphia*'s courtroom sequences, while they do segue into certain dramatic scenes, add no appreciable drama to the film; they often feel like the kind of dead spots that Demme always works so assiduously to avoid. Moreover, we never see Andy moving from denial to acceptance

Miguel and Andy at the home of Andy's parents

of his impending death, another example of deficiency in character-ization. Demme shares responsibility for these faults with scriptwriter Ron Nyswaner, who demonstrates here (in contrast to his script for *Swing Shift*) that he has a greater affinity for action than for commu-nicating subtle nuances of character. Yet we must also fault Demme and Nyswaner for apparently knowing very little about lawyers or the law. It's absurd for the film to have Andy's secretary assert that she can't evaluate his performance as a lawyer; indeed, it's often a lawyer's secretary who knows his or her work best. And though Andy's cred-ibility is brought up numerous times by defense attorney Belinda Conine (Mary Steenburgen) as some supposed indicator of his testi-mony's validity, it's clear that with respect to the trial, Andy's credi-bility as a lawyer is never in question. Nor is the credibility of Wyant, Wheeler at issue; it's never demonstrated in the film that despite their apparent prejudice and homophobia, any of the firm's partners made it known to any of the other partners that they suspected Andy had AIDS. And finally, when we see the jury deliberating, all that they focus on is the high esteem within which Andy was held in the firm, a fac-tor that has absolutely nothing to do with the issue that is at the trial's center: whether or not Andy was dismissed wrongfully, a point that hinges on the validity of the firm's assertion that Andy misplaced a very important case file and that he hadn't lived up to the partners' expectations (a contention at odds with his promotion to senior associate).

Andy and Joe during the trial

Although the jury finds for Andy, their verdict is not only problematic but unfounded. It's never established that anyone in Andy's law firm who suspected that he had AIDS conspired to make him seem incompetent. During the trial, however, Walter Kenton makes a distinction that's important to the film. Kenton talks about a woman in his former law firm who contracted AIDS as a result of a blood transfusion, and states that she got the disease "through no fault of [her] own." It's a point that draws attention to what some people seem to feel about AIDS: that it's a judgment against gays (in the words of one of the protester's signs outside the courtroom, "AIDS cures homosexuality," although since "AIDS" here translates into "death," one might say that death cures all physical conditions, which is a pointless and truistic assertion).

Nevertheless, the question of culpability with regard to the contraction of AIDS highlights a vital issue in the film. In her opening remarks, Belinda Conine says that Andy's "lifestyle, his reckless behavior, has cut short his life." Is she referring exclusively to his being gay? At first, it doesn't appear so. In her later examination of Andy, she asks him if he takes risks, by which question she is drawing attention to the way that he operates as a lawyer. Andy says that all good lawyers take risks. But then Conine personalizes the question's focus, pointing out that despite his knowing that it might weaken his immune system, Andy continued working long hours in a high stress job. However, Andy's curtailing his activities at Wyant, Wheeler would have been impossible; he would have had to change jobs in order to survive, an issue that, it is implied, he resolved by deciding to remain with the firm. In other words, he chose to live a certain way knowing that it would hasten his death, a clear demonstration of what could either be considered headstrong determination or, more likely given Andy's situation, imprudent behavior that seems like the playing out of a death wish.

Conine further affirms the point that she's making by relating Andy's behavior to his gay lifestyle, asking him if he ever attended the Stallion Showcase cinema, a gay movie theatre where, Andy admits, he had sex with a total stranger. This tryst occurred in 1984 or 1985; since this is the only sexual encounter Andy is shown to have outside of his relationship with Miguel (who is, as Andy points out, disease-free), the film implies that this is how Andy contracted AIDS. Further, there's the suggestion that this encounter represented a severe moral lapse for Andy, who was living in what appears to be a monogamous relationship with Miguel at the time (both Andy and Miguel wear what look like identical gold bands on their left hands' third fingers). *Philadelphia* implies that Andy's being unfaithful to Miguel occasioned a karmic judgment against him that took the form of AIDS. Indeed, just as *Philadelphia* shows the Demme ellipsis coming full circle against the firm of Wyant, Wheeler by having them lose the case and suffer not only a substantial monetary judgment but also face the possibility of their contracts with the city being terminated, the film also assigns fault for Andy's contracting AIDS. And though it's virtually inconceivable that the defense team could have found out about Andy's liaison at the gay theatre, it's nonetheless true that Andy's promiscuity *is* evidence of reckless behavior, and that despite his assertion that in 1984 or 1985 gays were aware of "a gay plague, a gay cancer" but didn't know how it was transmitted, there was information at the time to strongly recommend a sensible approach to sex. But then, for viewers to condemn *Philadelphia* for allowing Andy to make this unsupported assertion is to assume that the film is defending the comment instead of demonstrating how incognizant of some issues Andy chooses to be. In any case, many gays continued to have indiscriminate, unprotected sex right through the late 1980s and early 1990s; some probably still do, and it's just such behavior that *Philadelphia* places itself in opposition to.

Like Joe, Andy reveres the law. In response to Joe's question about what he loves about the law, Andy states, "Every now and again, not often but occasionally, you get to be a part of justice being done. That really is quite a thrill when that happens," thereby pointing up the fact that the more essential justice in which the film believes is people's right to equal treatment. It's far from Stanley Krameresque of Demme to assert that even in 1990s America, gays are often not treated equitably, or to imply that Charles Wheeler's reference to the "rules" in the Old and New Testaments suggests a condemnation of homosexuality that may have been translated into action.[13] Another issue that the film raises, that of self-perception, is present in the scene in which Andy is on the stand and first Belinda Conine and then Joe Miller ask him about the visibility of his lesions while he was working at Wyant, Wheeler. Despite Andy's protest that during the time in question the lesions on his face were quite perceptible to others, the film has Conine try to prove by virtue of the fact that Andy's current facial lesions cannot be seen that the senior law partners could not have known by appearances that Andy had AIDS (an extremely debatable point, since one of the partners and one of the firm's paralegals noticed shifts in Andy's weight and energy that suggested he had the disease). However, in something of a dramatic ploy, Joe has Andy open his shirt to show the lesions on his body, which, except for a brief glimpse of them, are not directly depicted, but are shown reflected in the mirror that Joe is holding, the same mirror that Conine had held up to Andy.[14] The point being made seems to be that perhaps more important than the direct perception of the lesions is society's view of them, here present in the analogous form of the mirror reflection. Sickness and debility often occasion repugnance, and one can't fault the defendants in the case for averting their eyes when the lesions are revealed. Yet it's also true that the real issue here is not the partners' abhorrence or fear of AIDS so much as the manner in which they may have treated someone whom they possibly suspected had the disease; it's the shift from apprehension about the disease to the loss of compassion toward someone who has it that Demme is underscoring.

Like many other Demme films, *Philadelphia* is less about its ostensible subject than it is about the issues that its subject brings up. What the film is primarily dealing with is the nature of commitment to life. That it chooses to deal with this issue via the subject of AIDS may indicate less a concern with gays than with the nature of the disease itself and the fact that unlike some cancers, AIDS is an illness that currently admits of no cure (it isn't even certain if the use of AZT has any appreciable effect on the disease's course). AIDS patients, then, live under a sentence of death that admits of no reprieve, and it's only through the type of communal bonding that the film periodically depicts that an otherwise intolerable situation is made a bit endurable. As we might expect, although it doesn't dwell on the horrors of AIDS, *Philadelphia* doesn't flinch from depicting them, as the glimpse of an AIDS-afflicted man at the AZT center makes plain. Nor does it avoid the distasteful aspects of its subject; Andy's "happy death"[15] is nothing like that of Camille in the Garbo film or Debra Winger in *Terms of Endearment*, to take two prominent examples of similar famous death scenes. In these films, what we're seeing isn't a romanticization of death so much as a misrepresentation of it. People simply don't die intact and beautiful as does Garbo's Camille; nor do they wave goodbye just before expiring as Winger does in *Terms*. At the end, Andy has lost all of his hair, and can scarcely breathe. Demme spares us Andy's death scene, though, and this is quite appropriate, since it would be difficult to represent without either falling into cliché or being too graphic.

Klawans felt that the swirling camera work and shifts in lighting in the scene during which Andy is listening to an aria from *Andrea Chenier* are inexcusable.[16] But then, as in Andy's family reunion, are we seeing an objective representation of reality here or the depiction of an emotional state of mind? In any case, objections to the scene overlook the fact that for many people on the brink of death, awareness, especially the awareness of one's distance from life, becomes preternaturally heightened. In such circumstances, music can have an almost overpowering effect, one that other people around you may very well be unable to comprehend (as is the case with Joe during the scene). And what is the essence of Andy's reaction? It's the perception of the beauty and sensuousness of a life from which he is slowly receding, and the realization that he is moving toward a death that constitutes the basis of an ineffable heartbreak for which all of the loving and compassionate family and friends in the world can't compensate. As *Philadelphia* implies, too many people, caught up in the circumstances of living from day to day, don't take the time to cherish their lives and those of the people around them. At one point, Andy says to Miguel, "you are worried we don't have very much time left," an assertion that Miguel, himself like Andy to a degree in denial, rejects. However, the point being made in Andy's remark doesn't apply solely to Andy and Miguel. Who, even those who are healthy, has anything other than a severely, sadly limited amount of time?

So let's forget the film's periodic awkwardness and occasionally slack pacing, the implausible drugstore scene, Andy's histrionic collapse in the courtroom, the holes of logic in the jury's reasoning, and Demme's perhaps too earnest attempt to make a "serious" statement about AIDS. What really matters in this film is its emotional truth. When family and friends come together after Andy's death, with Neil Young's song "Philadelphia" playing in the background telling about the "city of brotherly love, place I call home, don't turn your back on me, I don't want to be alone," we see both from the photo of Andy and Miguel on the candle-adorned table and the touching home videos that people are watching that Andy wasn't alone, that no one who really mattered ever turned his or her back on him, that he dies in the bosom of his family and in almost biblical fashion has been gathered unto his people with a compassion and understanding that all of us would want for ourselves. The goodness and love that Andy showed, the gentleness of his nature, the tenderness of his affection for Miguel—all of these qualities come back around to buoy him up when he most needs support. At the film's end, even Joe Miller is there,[17] his sympathetic presence demonstrating a change in his attitude toward gays that began with his appearance at Andy's party. The Demme circle closes on *Philadelphia*, which redeems *Silence of the Lambs*'s ethical lapse in a very satisfactory way.

Appendixes

Notes

Filmography

Bibliography

Index

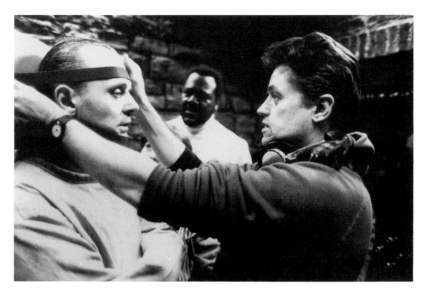

Anthony Hopkins, Frankie Faison, and Jonathan Demme on the set of *The Silence of the Lambs*

On Set and Beyond

An Interview with Jonathan Demme

Although some of *The Silence of the Lambs* was shot on location—for example, the scenes at the FBI training center in Quantico, Virginia—its central sequences, those involving the Baltimore interviews between Lecter and Starling and the basement pursuit of Jame Gumb, were shot by Demme on the third floor of a warehouse on the outskirts of Pittsburgh. In March, 1990, we visited the film's set.

After reaching the third floor and passing through a temporary wooden doorway, you emerge into a large, high-ceilinged room in which set flats have been constructed; to the side, an oubliette has been sunk into the floor. At the bottom of the oubliette there's a stuffed toy dog—obviously the stand-in for Gumb's poodle, Precious.

The set for Gumb's basement is laid out just as it is described in Thomas Harris's book. It's a series of narrow, dark, low-ceilinged, interconnected rooms. One room contains a stainless steel dissecting table, fish tanks with neon green fluid in them in which "skin" is curing, rows of surgical instruments, and glass cases filled with moths. There's a dingy passageway leading to the bathroom, in which a plaster corpse of a dead old woman with stringy gray hair and wrinkled skin is lying submerged in the tub. In order to shoot Clarice's point of view of the room's corpse, the Steadicam operator has to squeeze his way into the bathroom. To give him more leeway for another shot of the room, the bathtub, corpse and all, is removed. Ten minutes later, a lit cigarette appears in the corpse's outstretched hand, a crew member's idea of a grim joke.

On one of the walls, Gumb has tacked up a map of the United States, probably to determine the drop sites for his victims' bodies. Another hallway leads to Gumb's living room, which contains a sewing machine and dressmaker dummies with "leather" fittings hanging off them. One of the room's walls features shots of Gumb posing with strippers and garishly dressed prostitutes (the photos are just barely visible in the film). The feeling here is one of claustrophobia and clutter.

The set has been made to look dirty, and when you're in it, there's not much room to maneuver. On the other side of the flats, technicians are carrying props, or setting up and adjusting sound equipment. A camera operator is rehearsing the point-of-view shot of Starling looking down the steps to Gumb's basement before she begins the descent into his private hell.

Jonathan Demme is a very gracious man; he makes you feel like he's glad you're here, that this isn't merely some duty of cordiality he is carrying out. Everyone on set refers to him as either Jonathan or JD. The crew is one big accessible group. When we remark on the set's relaxed atmosphere, Demme responds that his people are all hand-picked, not only for their expertise but for their affability as well.

In accordance with union rules, cinematographer Tak Fujimoto never handles the camera; operators manipulate it, constantly lining up shots, trying new angles, and watching the playback on a video monitor. Orders for retakes come from assistant director Ron Bozman; Demme watches and makes comments. Production coordination has been handled by Kenneth Utt (who plays the dour FBI agent in *Married to the Mob* and the rural doctor in *Lambs*) and Edward Saxon, who had a bit part in *Something Wild* and played the Hare Krishna whose finger is broken by Alec Baldwin's Junior Frenger in *Miami Blues*. Saxon says that when they were shooting the scene with the moths flying around Gumb's basement, some couldn't be captured and for days were loose on set. We try to convince Saxon that there's one crawling on his back, but he doesn't fall for the joke. "Too many people have tried that one on me already," he says.

It takes Demme about fourteen hours to shoot two minutes worth of action today. By dinner, which occurs at seven o'clock, everyone is looking a bit ragged, so Demme breaks out some surprises: *Silence of the Lambs* shorts and tee shirts emblazoned with moths, one of which is bright red. To relieve the inevitable tension of working on a film like this one, Tak Fujimoto puts his shorts on over his pants, after which it's back to work. Three months later we talked to Demme in New York, where he was finishing the film's final sound mix.

B: How did you get involved with *Silence of the Lambs*?

D: The screenplay was already in the works when I read the book. Gene Hackman had wanted to direct it and be in it so Orion bought the book for him. As I understand it he had reservations about the violence in the material and withdrew from the project. Ted Tally had been working on the screenplay for many weeks by then; Orion gave me the book to read and I loved it. I knew enough about Ted Tally to know that the script was going to be very good so I committed to do it before even reading the script, which turned out to be great. I'm always looking for a good script. They're so hard to find. That's why many movies are so bad nowadays.

B: You've said that you don't write good scripts.

D: No. I can come up with the occasional idea or scene but that's all. I'm not a good writer—alas. It would make things so much easier.

B: Even with *Something Wild* in mind, this film seems to be quite a departure in tone for you.

D: This is the most serious film I've ever done. It's about a social problem, serial killers, who are a product of a society that tolerates epidemic child abuse. We don't get into the child abuse dimension very much in the film, but it's part of the film's feel, part of Clarice's background although she's suppressed it. Now, I love comedy, and it's very challenging to make comedy work and I like that challenge. The mood I'm in at this moment in my life, though, is that there are so many other subjects that urgently need creative examination. This isn't a time for laughing; this is a time for digging into some of these issues and putting them in people's faces. Although if a script came along that was a hilarious comedy . . .

B: What kind of visual mood were you searching for with this film?

D: My big concern was to avoid the typical great shadowy thriller look because stories like this in which the lonely law enforcement person is tracking the terrifying killer can overuse effects like long shadows. I really didn't want to employ the traditional prose of the thriller, which I was trying to get away from. I was fascinated by *Rosemary's Baby*, which I look at a lot. It's a very very bright movie. I said to Tak, let's make this film bright. Of course there are times when we won't be able to make it bright, the basement scenes for example, but as much as possible, let's allow the audience to see everything. That will emphasize the dread of the dark when it happens. And let's not feel that we have to visually juice up the film with ominous shadows. We'll let the story and the characters be ominous.

Tak took that one step further. He said, Okay, let's not go the strong, righteous, traditional thriller look, but let's not just brighten everything up either. He wanted to bring a certain kind of light to the scenes, a kind of Vittorio Storaro type of lighting, which pleases Tak.

B: Yet audiences still react to traditional visual cues, feeling that dark is ominous and light is safe.

D: Well, it works in life; if you come home and it's dark in your house and you turn all the lights on, you cheer up the mood.

B: Does the Hitchcock camera style enter in here, something you used in *Last Embrace*?

D: Yes. You've already seen enough of this movie to appreciate to what an overwhelming degree I steal Hitchcock's style. In *Last Embrace*, which I can't watch, I was kind of wallowing in style. I went into that movie thinking, Okay, here's a Hitchcockian thriller, and a lot of energy went into style more than into content. In some scenes where the camera should have been in the actors' faces, when they were really communicating what they had to say to the audience, the camera was in an extremely wide position drinking in the environment. I put too much emphasis into the character of the locations and not enough into the characters.

Now, though, I understand the Hitchcock style. I'm not trying to copy it; I'm using it in a fashion that I understand. I understand the style's strengths, I know when to employ it, and I've embraced it more and more in my own quiet way, not necessarily in terms of visual flamboyance but more in the use of subjective camera and how to photograph actors to communicate story and character points.

I also wanted a distinctive sound texture to this film. I'm always trying to do the best sound track of all time. Sound is a very important factor, one that audiences always feel, which is why I work so closely with the sound designer. The film's music enters in here, too. We're surrounded by music in our everyday lives, whether we program it or someone else does. It affects our mood, so I like to play with that element. *Something Wild* represents my most compulsive involvement with the music track. But it's not just a question of stringing together popular songs on the sound track. It's the idea that music affects us so strongly on an emotional level that fascinates me.

B: *Married to the Mob*'s violence seemed distanced somehow, an effect that we assumed was intentional.

D: Well, I did do it intentionally and that's the cineaste in me but as the critic of violent movies I sit back and think, hmmm.

B: How do you resolve that dilemma, especially with *Lambs*, which almost seems to revel in violence?

D: I think it's important to show that violence is truly awful. The struggle I have, which I don't think is present in this movie at all but is in *Married to the Mob*, is that even with my aversion to violence, the cineaste in me can't, for example, resist having Dean Stockwell come tumbling out of his car using a two-gun style to decimate guys in a scene that I hope looks like it's out of some Raoul Walsh movie from the forties. I also understand that in a sheer pleasure movie like *Married to the Mob*, it's important to entertain the audience. There I'm trying to walk a tightrope between making it exciting and not making it fun. I think I failed there; I fell into fun. In that Burger World scene, the shot of Chris Isaak shooting his guns off gets away from the discipline of trying to show violence as awful and falls into the male fantasy of how thrilling gunplay is. I'm not pleased with that, although I still enjoy those scenes. I'm very schizo on the subject. It's easier for me to enjoy that kind of material in other movies than it is in my own.

I have similar problems with sex and nudity in movies. I enjoy sex and nudity if they're presented in a—I want to try to be honest and say in a provocative way, in a compelling way. However, more and more I see the nudity and sex in movies as exploitative, especially of women, and I'm trying very much to fight against that. I think that it's fine to have nudity and sex in movies where that's truly the subject matter but I think it's important to have male nudity as well as female nudity just to be democratic and egalitarian.

B: There's no nudity in *Lambs* but the film certainly is violent. What's your attitude towards the film's bloody scenes?

D: In this movie the violence is horrifying, the buildups are exciting. I hope they put people on edge. But the payoffs aren't fun. There's not some orgasmic spray of machine gun bullets. Even in our climax, where the heroine is finally squared off with the bad guy, she shoots him and it's awful. The audience isn't invited to cheer. I didn't want to boil this film down to a ''and then she got her gun and blew the bad guy away'' story. The camera never sees relief on Clarice's face after she shoots Gumb; there's not a cut to her which lets you go ''Yay!'' You see Gumb's awful, slow death and she's appalled by it.

B: Are you pleased with the film's casting?

D: I've had the good fortune to work with terrific actresses time and time again. Coming off of any given movie, especially a recent one, you want to work with all of the gifted people you've worked with before. Michelle Pfeiffer and I had a superb time making *Married to the Mob* and we were both trying to find something so we could continue working together because we thought we had just scratched the surface of our potential in that film. Exceptional actress that she is, Michelle was my first choice for Clarice but the material proved too strong for her.

B: I'm not sure that she could have been as assertive as Clarice should be.

D: Had she played this part she would have become that for you. Michelle agreed to do the film but she couldn't deal with the violence, which is the same thing that Gene Hackman had experienced. It was just too violent for Michelle, too dark. I thought that was unfortunate because I think it is a misconception of the material, that in fact the light of the Clarice character is ultimately more powerful than the darkness of the story. Jodie was already familiar with the material and loved it. She's very strong in the part, which proves that if you don't get your first choice it doesn't mean you're not going to get a 10.

B: From the outset did you want Anthony Hopkins for the part of Lecter?

D: Yes, he was the first person I felt really strongly about, although every actor age thirty and up wanted to play Hannibal Lecter. There was such competition for that part; it was unbelievable. The thing that's so exciting about working with these great actors, and with a man like Tak Fujimoto, is that they are gifted artists, so you know that what they're going to do will be extraordinary but you don't know what it's going to be like. It's endlessly thrilling. You see a similar split later on. The movie on the screen never bears the faintest resemblance to the movie in your head. Starting out, you always think you know what the film's going to look like, what it's going to feel like, but you really haven't a clue. It's terrifying but true. It took me a couple of movies to get used to that. I was disappointed for a while; I couldn't tell the qualitative difference between that "perfect version" I had in my head and the reality of trying to make a movie until I realized that the one I carried around in my head is just like some kind of tool you have until the real thing comes along.

B: I found myself liking the Lecter character in the film and the book.

D: That's one of the aspects of this movie, one of the things that disturbed me up front, the idea that Lecter's so likable. One of the wonderful things about the art of telling a great yarn—I'm talking about Thomas Harris here—is that you can still break the rules, you can have a character so complicated that he's kind of lovable, and you will experience him doing horrific things that truly repel you, but at the end of the day you may still like him. I've given up trying to rationalize all of that. Yet it wasn't a problem in the film; it was only a problem on paper.

B: It seems to me that it's still a problem for the film, because you wind up liking Lecter despite what he does. In fact, I think a lot of people will tend to cheer him on when he begins planning revenge for the wrongs that have been done to him.

D: Well, you're going a little too far for me. I don't want to condone people wanting to see an innocent get killed. Yet at our last preview, when the audience simply roared its approval at the cut that showed what Lecter was about to do to Chilton, I was thrilled.

B: It's not clear to me why Lecter became such a homicidal person to begin with.

D: My belief, as a fan of the book, and as someone who's carefully watched Tony's portrayal of Lecter, is that here's a person who is so much smarter than everybody else that over the course of time he's been bored to repulsion by people's limitations and has finally turned on everyone in a uniquely dreadful yet, for him, kind of fun way.

B: The editing on this movie reminds me of the editing on *Married to the Mob*; both films are extremely lean, to the extent that there's really no point in the film during which you can leave the theater, even for a moment, without missing something interesting. Is this an important quality for you?

D: Sure. If the movie doesn't have a pace that works, all of the good characters in the world won't do you any good. Actually, *Melvin and Howard* was the last film that I had difficulty taking material out of.

B: Difficult in the sense that you ultimately didn't take the material out?

D: I did take it out, but with great agony. You don't say, "Oh, I love that scene, I hate to lose it" so much as you realize that with that scene out of there the picture moves along in a way that will be far more agreeable to the audience.

B: What was edited out of *Melvin and Howard*?

D: There was a scene in which Melvin and Little Red run out of gas by the Mustang Ranch and Melvin went inside and had a funny and sweet scene with one of the hookers who makes love to him for free because he's so cute and charming. There was a wonderful four-minute scene between Paul Le Mat and Charlene Colt who was a lonely housewife on his milk route who invites him in, and there were lots of scenes between Melvin and Linda after they broke up.

B: How involved do you get in your films' editing?

D: Intimately. I work with Craig [McKay] and let him have a full whack at the footage without my telling Craig the ways that I want the footage used. I'll never tell the editor how to cut a scene because he or she may find a more exciting approach to it than I could ever dream up.

B: Is there a certain editing rhythm that you strive for?

D: I don't really have an active aesthetic about that. I just have an emotional response to the current movie and a concern that the story move fast enough and that the characters come across.

B: You see a lot of *Married to the Mob*'s outtakes at the film's end.

Some of them look great, such as the one in which Michelle Pfeiffer and Carol East are talking after hours at the beauty parlor.

D: It's true, that was a really sweet scene. They're talking about Michelle's upcoming date with Matthew Modine. It was really nice to see her get down and hear how nervous she was about the date, but it slowed the movie down. You could feel it as you were watching it, and at that point we hadn't provided any big events lately which you need in this type of film. After all, *Married To the Mob*'s story is as light as a feather; you have to beware of how much time you take telling it. If I sit there and get bored watching scenes that I've worked on and loved, how on earth can I expect you guys to enjoy them? It wasn't easy, though; we had to fight to get the film down to the right length.

B: And that final tango between Modine and Pfeiffer?

D: That's a reward to the stalwarts who stayed to the very end.

B: Your films usually have a pronounced political stance. Was there a problem with communicating that in *Silence of the Lambs*?

D: No, because I'm pretty sure that over the years I've come to understand to what extent social concerns, more than political attitudes, can benefit a movie. But I know where you need to draw the line before it starts becoming intrusive and turning off the vast majority of the audience. Movies need to have a social responsibility, though, and I certainly try to have that present in the films that I do, but I'm also careful not to go overboard with it. Most of our production company energy now is directed at trying to develop films that in some way would have appeal to racially mixed audiences. We're looking for black subjects, racial subjects, interracial subjects. We want to make movies that have strong appeal to audiences other than just white people.

B: Are you hoping that this film is going to be an explosive financial success?

D: Yes, deeply. I want the people who put their choices on the line and finance the movies I direct to be rewarded for their choices. I work because of them and I want them to prosper because of my work. The money this movie makes is an index of how many people saw and, in theory, enjoyed the movie. For a while there I thought, you're sort of doing it for yourself; it's such a thrill, it's so exciting, as long as it has integrity, who cares? That's an early phase. But I do want a lot of people to see this film; I'm not just making it for the fun of it. It's still fun, but that's not why it's being made.

B: Do you think there's a potential contradiction between the kind of filmmaking that you do and overt financial success?

D: I hope not.

B: It occurred to me the other day that because you're so willing to let other people speak through what you do, as in *Stop Making Sense*, you may efface yourself while you're doing that.

D: Well, in some cases I think you need to; in *Swimming to Cambodia*, that was my job.

B: But it may preclude success for you.

D: You know what? I still get profit checks on *Stop Making Sense*; it's the only movie I've ever had them on. Anyway, that's not likely to happen if the band is as great as Talking Heads, or if the storyteller is as gifted as Spalding. For those kinds of films, the challenge is to very literally make the movie audience get as excited about their performance as I was initially.

B: Then what happens to the Demme style?

D: Audiences don't really give a damn about that anyway. The vast majority of moviegoers want to have a good time, want to be moved or provoked. That's why I like to do so many different kinds of things, like documentaries and music videos, because you can keep demonstrating your interest and appreciation. It's a very personal thing to make a documentary on a subject. I'm making a documentary now for Spanish TV about my cousin, who's a minister at a church in Harlem.[1] We've been shooting it off and on for about a year. That film doesn't have to make a lot of money. There I can just wallow in what interests me about this man, not because he's my cousin but because of what he does and what he thinks. The Haiti documentary [*Haiti: Dreams of Democracy*] was kind of like that too. I had fallen in love with these people and this country and I was able to aim a camera at the things that I adored and film them. But the great thrill, no matter what kind of movie it is, is to have the story on film really work for people on its own merits.

| Cutting It Right
An Interview
with Craig McKay

Craig McKay has been the editor on most of Jonathan Demme's films since 1976. A member of American Cinema Editors, McKay has also edited *Miami Blues*, *She-Devil*, and the award-winning television mini-series *Holocaust*, for which he received an Emmy. He was an assistant editor on *The Exorcist*, worked with Warren Beatty on *Reds*, and recently edited director David Seltzer's film *Shining Through*. A month after the Chicago preview of *Silence of the Lambs*, I spoke to McKay about his work with Jonathan Demme.

B: There appears to be something of a conflict between what I would refer to as a traditional editing style and the more free-wheeling type of cutting that Jonathan Demme wants in his films. How is this contradiction worked out?

M: The styles seem to be at odds with each other but I don't think they really are. I start off with something I've always called my European cut, which is long; everything is in it. Then we start to tighten. Jonathan and I have this expression, that "the film will speak," that it will go through what we call "The Process" and end up telling us what it needs. Since we both like to tell a story with brevity, we find a meeting ground where the film fulfills all of my classical requirements and yet it's open and not so traditional in terms of film grammar.

What I like to do is be on the moment. In other words, that when something is happening, you're seeing it happen. That's the primary line of the narrative. Then there are other areas, like going for reactions, which are usually secondary unless it's important for the narrative line for those things to be up front. The film's first cut establishes the right time and the right place for the narrative. We then embellish it by putting in some more detail. Usually, what happens is that we end up inserting more cuts as we go along.

B: At what point do you enter into the production?

Scott Glenn's Jack Crawford outside FBI headquarters in a scene cut from *The Silence of the Lambs* after the studio previews

M: I start on the first day of shooting. Jonathan shoots on Monday, I get the film on Tuesday, and I start cutting after he looks at it. The important thing is that Jonathan have his first draft of the movie a week or two after shooting is completed. There's material in this cut that isn't going to remain, or that's going to be used differently. In *Silence of the Lambs*, for example, there are many scenes in which I've taken the end of a scene and made it work as the beginning of a scene. For example, there's the scene in which Lecter talks with Clarice about one of Buffalo Bill's victims. The scene originally opened with the line, "Were they all large girls, big through the hips, roomy?" but Jonathan and I felt that the point of the scene was to start on Clarice offering her deal right away, so I placed some of the other dialogue later in the scene.

Then there's a scene in which Clarice is interviewing one of Federica Bimmel's friends at a drugstore. The first line in that scene now was originally the last line, "What's it like being an FBI agent?" We moved it up front because it seemed to make the scene work better. Editing is often like rewriting dialogue.

B: But after the Chicago preview you also dropped scenes, for example the one in the FBI official's office in which he suspends Clarice, and the scene in which Crawford gives Clarice money so she can go to Belvedere.

M: Yes, that last scene got a good reaction in the preview but it wasn't working for us. It felt more like exposition than action and at that point in the movie we wanted something that would give us a push forward.

B: The way you have the film edited currently, though, Clarice doesn't really seem like a renegade.

M: That's right. However, what Clarice does now is act on her own initiative, and that was an option we all felt was better for the movie. When she determines to go to Belevedere on her own, in the face of her suspension and Crawford being taken off the case, well, that material wasn't strong. That's supposed to be what we call in the business a strong curtain: she's left out in the cold with no place to go. But you never felt that she was really excluded because she was still working on the case.

B: What struck me watching you work is how malleable a film's scenes are. You can do so many things: alter the background ambient sound, use different dialogue takes. It occurred to me that actors get a significant amount of help from editors.

M: Yes, but you need that raw material to begin with, and you also need to respect your responsibility to deliver the emotional lines, the narrative arcs. Filmmaking does rely on a lot of people. The thing that I do is to build performances.

B: Jonathan said that you really respect what the actors do and that you work extremely hard to make sure that what's on screen is the best they had to give.

M: Absolutely, and this is where Jonathan and I are on common ground. From working with Jonathan for twelve years I know that his priority in terms of storytelling is character. He protects his characters; they're sacred. They're even more sacred to him than the narrative. It's the characters that attract Jonathan to a story, that make him want to do it. We both respect them and respect making those characters come alive, creating the best performance. However, Jonathan is becoming more involved in the narrative line. If you look at the distance between *Melvin and Howard* and *Silence of the Lambs*, you can see that. *Melvin* is just this character piece; there is no narrative. That film is hung on gossamer.

B: That's also the case with *Married to the Mob*. Jonathan said that the story's so light, it almost floats away.

M: That's true. There's a heavy emphasis on character in that movie. The characters in that film are overwhelming, and that, for me, is Jonathan's gift. When Jonathan says, "This is the movie I want to do and these are the characters," I know on the deepest level that he is committed to these people.

B: But you said that Jonathan's work has changed.

M: *Silence of the Lambs* certainly has a strong narrative line and strong characters, as you know. When you open a story you promise to tell about a certain character. If you don't fulfill that promise you upset a lot of people. That's what happened with *Something Wild*. The promise was to tell you a story about Charlie Driggs but you get caught up with the character of Ray, who's very seductive and very dark, and with Lulu, and though the film eventually ends up being Charlie's story, there are moments when you drift.

Silence of the Lambs doesn't do that. It has an incredible set-up. You're not going anywhere once you hear that Clarice is going into the asylum to interview Lecter. As simple as it is, that scene in Crawford's office sucks you in as effectively as the opening of the original *Invasion of the Body Snatchers* does, which in terms of getting you into the story is one of the fastest movies to engage an audience that's ever been made.

B: When you're working with material that's violent, as it is in *Lambs*, and you see a scene over and over again, do you tend to become distanced from it?

M: No. What I've learned to do, what you're trained to do, is to always remember your first impression. Quite frankly, a lot of my decisions are made when I look at dailies for the first time. Whether I can continue to do that once I get to the editing stage is another question.

B: So for you there isn't a significant difference between working on *Lambs* and working on a film like *Married to the Mob*?

M: No. When I sit down to edit, I'm going through the motions of storytelling. I'm looking at the material much differently than an audience does. I'm saying to myself, "Do I need this reaction shot for this piece of information?; Is this point clear here?; Am I giving the audience the right information at the right time?" Editing involves that kind of orchestrating. I'm doing what a writer would do. A writer varies sentences; I vary shots. You can't have them all the same rhythm. But more than that is how the audience is getting the story. When you break the film down piece by piece, it's not like sitting there and watching a scene play. And yes, *Lambs* is a hard film, a dark tale. I've worked on a lot of hard films. I was an assistant editor on the original *Exorcist*. Linda Blair was puking pea soup all the time, but I concentrated on my work. I had a different experience when I was doing *Holocaust*. That film affected me quite deeply. In fact, I don't think anything has gotten to me as strongly as that. The subject just took me over.

B: What would happen if you started feeling that there was indulgence to the violence, that it was being celebrated, that an attitude like that was embedded in the material?

M: But I think it's true about this movie. Now, it's easy to make a gore movie; it's easy to make a fast action film in which twenty people get killed in ten seconds. That's the simplest thing in the world. What Jonathan does with this movie is to make that experience a really human experience. *Lambs* makes you say, wait a minute, Lecter is seductive and alluring but he's not one of them, he's one of us.

B: Still, the biggest sock in the film is the ending when Lecter says, "I'm having an old friend for dinner," and then you see Chilton. The statement seems to celebrate revenge and tends to validate Lecter's mode of action.

M: It's not even a moral issue with me and I'll tell you why. Lecter says it himself when Chilton is listening in. He talks about abuse, and he talks about what it does. In a sense, he talks about how evil abuse is. Lecter also talks about how Chilton is abusing him. As you've said, all of Jonathan's films operate for the most part on a very simple premise, the old adage, "what goes around comes around."

B: You're saying this applies to Chilton. But doesn't this apply to Lecter as well?

M: Well, it applies to the animal that we created, that this culture created. There are aberrations in culture, and when you talk about child abuse, you're also talking about its results. Even among the most intelligent people you can see how abuse distorts. Any one of us could be that dark soul.

Jon really throws stuff at you. He challenges you, more so than anybody I've ever worked for. There's a scene in this movie that didn't exist in the book, the one in which Gumb is making himself up and dancing. Basically, they shot some second unit material and Jon said, do something with it. For me, that scene is, editorially, a leap. It comes out of traditional roots and then makes a leap beyond them. "Fuck me, would you fuck me, I'd fuck me . . . " It's a very dark scene.

It's interesting because some part of you has to be very stable before you can work with some of this material; it can get to you. When I went into this film I knew it was an extraordinarily dark tale. But I also knew that I had better recognize that a large part of this darkness is part of me, too, and that I need to own up to it. This is part of what we are capable of doing. Lecter is a character who revels in his darkness, and that's a part of us.

B: Yes. When Anthony Hopkins is asking Clarice for disclosures, he's leaning back, drinking it all in, vampirically, yet he also seems to be doing therapy on Clarice.

M: It's not really healing, though. Lecter takes Clarice into her own darkness but doesn't do anything with it except use it to get off on.

B: It's interesting that the film's violence isn't really that graphic.

M: Most of it is played off camera with the exception of the most important example of violence, which is Lecter's unveiling: the attack on the policemen. Usually, Jon represents violence indirectly. At the beginning of *Married to the Mob* a man gets shot in the head but you don't see the violence; you see its result. Jon is able to represent violence in such a way that he doesn't diminish its impact and yet he doesn't sensationalize it. In the original cut of the *Lambs* jailhouse murder scene, I had the beating going on twice as long. But I saw Jonathan squirming in his seat in the screening room and I knew he wasn't going to buy it.

I've worked with a lot of directors, but Jon is the most demanding. He's ruthless with his material in trying to edit it down. When it comes to the editing stage nothing is sacred. Aside from the scene in which Lecter has Clarice tell him the lambs story, there isn't a single scene in *Silence of the Lambs* that hasn't been worked inside out and upside down.

B: Jonathan told me that he was trying to do a lot of Hitchcock in this film.

M: Very much so. I think it's clear that there are influences. When Lecter is looking at the pen on his cot and we're moving in on Lecter's face, that's the kind of shot Hitchcock would have done, as is the overhead shot after the jailhouse murders. There's no doubt that Hitchcock is one of Jon's heroes; he absolutely worships the man.

I'll tell you a funny story. Jon and I were out at Universal Studios in Los Angeles working on *Melvin and Howard*. This was 1979. We'd just come out of the screening room and were going back to the cutting room. As we were crossing the road a limousine was coming down the hill and towards us. Over the dashboard you could see Hitchcock sitting in the front seat with his driver, but he's so short that you can just see his nose and his eyes and his forehead. As the limo is passing us, Jon is jumping up and down like a little boy, waving his hand and shouting, "Hi, Mr. Hitchcock! Hello, Mr. Hitchcock!" Hitchcock drove by and simply raised his hand and lowered it and the car drove on.

Like Hitchcock's work, Jon's movies are very tight, very lean. He also has a strong sense of camera. But most of all, it's his quirky, oddball characters that are unique to him. I don't know anybody else who's doing his kind of material. I think Jon is quite simply one of our originals.

Notes

Introduction

1. Corman himself uses the term "The Roger Corman Graduate School of Film" in Roger Corman and Jim Jerome, *How I Made a Hundred Movies in Hollywood and Never Lost a Dime* (New York: Random House, 1990), 235.

2. Demme acted as co-chair of Filmmakers United Against Apartheid.

3. Roy Blount, Jr., "Adventures in the Demme Monde," *Esquire*, Sept. 1988, 208.

4. Michael Sragow, "Jonathan Demme on the Line," *American Film*, Jan.-Feb. 1984, 45.

5. Ibid., 46.

6. Ibid.

7. Joshua Hammer, "Bio—Jonathan Demme," *People Weekly*, May 25, 1987, 100.

8. For more details on these excisions, see the interview with Craig McKay, appendix B.

9. Blount, "Adventures," 207.

10. Ibid., 214.

11. Interview with Jonathan Demme, New York, June 1990. The interview appears in this book as appendix A.

12. Ibid.

13. Gavin Smith, "Identity Check," *Film Comment* (Jan.-Feb. 1991): 29-30.

14. Anthony DeCurtis, "An Outsider in This Society: An Interview with Don DeLillo," in Frank Lentricchia, ed., *Introducing Don DeLillo* (Durham: Duke University Press, 1991), 48.

15. Ibid., 50.

16. Ibid., 52.

17. Don DeLillo, *Libra* (New York: Viking Publishers, 1988).

18. This type of characterization is a major feature of classic American literature, as Leslie Fiedler demonstrates in his *Love and Death in the American Novel* (New York: Dell Publishers, 1966).

19. *Philadelphia* inverts this trope's meaning. See chapter 11.

20. DeLillo, *Libra*, 12.

21. Demme interview, appendix A.

22. Northrop Frye, *A Natural Perspective* (New York: Harcourt, Brace, Jovanovich, 1965), 73.

23. Northrop Frye, *Anatomy of Criticism* (Princeton: Princeton University Press, 1971), 43.

24. Frye, *A Natural Perspective*, 74-75.

25. Ibid., 75.

26. Ibid., 75-76.

27. Ibid., 76.

28. Ibid.

29. In the film, only "Spider" escapes this pattern.

30. Frye, *A Natural Perspective*, 78.

31. In *Married to the Mob*, the statement appears as "everything that goes around comes around."

1. Canned Heat

1. The film was also released under the title *Renegade Girls*.

2. J. Philip di Franco, ed., *The Movie World of Roger Corman* (New York: Chelsea House, 1979), 55.

3. Corman has said that what he found interesting about this film is that it is from the outsiders' point of view rather than that of the community.

4. Blount, "Adventures," 214.

2. Road Crazies

1. Sragow, "Jonathan Demme," 46.

2. This clash between reality and emotional realism resurfaces in *Philadelphia*.

3. Radio Daze

1. In this discussion we have chosen to use the re-release title instead of the rather meaningless original release title of *Handle with Care*.

2. During this period, Peter Falk, who had seen and admired *Citizens Band*, gave Demme the opportunity to direct an episode of the television series "Colombo."

3. Ivan Doig's *Utopian America: Dreams and Realities* (New Jersey: Hayden Books, 1976) posits that in the United States, town names like Union and Paradise represent attempts at building communities based on utopian values.

4. Problems on the Set

1. Demme interview, appendix A.

2. Personal communication from Jonathan Demme to authors.

3. Demme interview, appendix A.

4. Blount, "Adventures," 214.

5. Sragow, "Jonathan Demme," 80.

6. Roger Corman has a bit role as the head of the MacBride plant.

7. In an interview published before the film's completion, Demme commented: "It's easy for us to sympathize in a big way with the women who were yanked out of one life-style, into a deep involvement with the fate of the world, and then summarily pulled out of what the world considered 'meaningfulness' and sent back to the home. But we complicate that by asking, 'What about the guys coming back? Did they not deserve to get their jobs and families back?' It's an unanswerable dilemma." Sragow, "Jonathan Demme," 80.

5. Huck Meets the Hucksters

1. Sragow, "Jonathan Demme," 80.

2. Demme also received the New York Film Critics Award for Best Director for the film.

3. Smith, "Identity Check," 37.

4. We use quotes around Hughes's name to emphasize the fact that the film leaves the actual identity of Jason Robards' character in question, this despite the fact that the character is identified as Howard Hughes in the end credits.

5. The scene's setting, and many of its details, seem derived from the Las Vegas marriage chapel ceremony between Melba and Joe Bob in *Crazy Mama*.

6. Imitation of Life

1. Demme also duplicates the technique from *Vertigo* in which Jimmy Stewart looks down the bell tower staircase and perspective increases before our eyes, a function of a simultaneous zoom back and dolly in.

7. Many People Clapping, One Man Rapping

1. The film received the National Society of Film Critics Award for Best Documentary.

2. Byrne designed the stage lighting and stage screens.

3. *Swimming to Cambodia*'s footage was filmed on three consecutive evenings before a live audience at Manhattan's Performing Garage in November 1986.

4. D. H. Lawrence, *Studies in Classic American Literature* (New York: Viking Press, 1964), 2.

5. Spalding Gray, *Swimming to Cambodia* (New York: Theatre Communications Group, 1985).

6. Alain Robbe-Grillet, *For a New Novel*, trans. Richard Howard (New York: Books for Libraries Press, n.d.), 45.

7. Kael notes a further objectionable aspect to the film: that Gray seems to be using the war as a way of making himself seem politically correct. The artificiality of this plea for moral rightness is something Demme

would never allow in his completely fictive films. Review of *Swimming to Cambodia*, *The New Yorker*, April 6, 1987, 84.

8. Thomas W. Benson and Carolyn Anderson, *Reality Fictions: The Films of Frederick Wiseman* (Carbondale: Southern Illinois University Press, 1989), 1.

8. Bicentennial Babies

1. For a full explication of this theme in American fiction, see Leslie Fiedler's *Love and Death in the American Novel*.

2. In this sense, the film dramatizes the denial of the repressed self that is endemic to classic horror films. See Robin Wood's essay "An Introduction to the American Horror Film" in *The American Nightmare* (Toronto: Festival of Festivals, 1971), 7-28.

3. Lulu's haircut and name obviously refer to the G. W. Pabst film *Pandora's Box* (1928), which starred Brooks as an impish dancer who seemed a locus for dark forces.

4. After Ray hits the clerk, part of the action is shown in slow motion, as is the shot of Lulu throwing the same gun that Ray had used during the robbery down a storm drain. The identical technique makes us linger on the violence that the gun has brought forth.

5. Charles Willeford, *Sideswipe* (New York: St. Martin's Press, 1987), 50, 54. It's possible that Demme may have been introduced to Willeford's work during the production of *Something Wild*. Later, Willeford's book *Miami Blues* became the basis for George Armitage's 1990 film of the same name.

6. Earlier, though, the handcuffs operated as a symbol of the developing intimacy between Lulu and Charlie. Just before entering Peaches' house, the following exchange between the characters, which affirms the handcuffs' symbolic importance, takes place.

Charlie: [Noticing that Lulu is unlocking the handcuffs] What are you doing?

Audrey: I'm setting you free.

Charlie: Maybe I don't want to be free.

Audrey: Maybe you're not.

7. Willeford, *Sideswipe*, 109.

8. This concern with who one really is is mirrored in Charlie's obsession with calling people by the names on their name-tags, an ironic concern with the reality of one's identity given that Charlie has been misrepresenting himself to Audrey throughout the film's first half.

9. Ecclesiastes, chap. 9, verse 4.

10. The phrase recalls *Who Am I This Time?*, which deals with the split between one's stage and real-life personae.

9. The Gang's All Here

1. Demme interview, appendix A.

2. Ibid.

3. The relationship between Jame Gumb and his dog Precious would fit this pattern were it not that the relationship is obviously pathological.

4. Tony's Wild West gun-twirling establishes another link between him and Mike, since over his bed, Mike has a poster of a cowboy riding a bucking horse.

5. The juxtaposition during a party sequence of elements associated with life versus death also occurs during Charlie and Audrey's dance at the reunion in *Something Wild*, in the midst of which Ray first appears.

10. Screams

1. Smith, "Identity Check," 30.

2. Ibid., 34.

3. Demme interview, appendix A.

4. Smith, "Identity Check," 33.

5. Ibid.

6. This scene's suggestive elements are duplicated later in the film when Clarice is in the funeral home and is surrounded by policemen who are all taller than she is.

7. This concern doubtless encouraged Demme to continue working on his next project, *Philadelphia*, which makes this issue central to its action.

8. Interestingly, this sound is twice duplicated by Lecter, first while he listens to Clarice's Plum Island offer, then when he watches Chilton search for his pen, which Lecter has appropriated. The similarity of sound draws attention to Lecter's selfish concern for his own freedom, even if it is to be purchased at the price of allowing Gumb to continue murdering women.

9. Thomas Harris, *The Silence of the Lambs* (New York: St. Martin's Press, 1988), 172.

10. The shot seems reminiscent of a line in T. S. Eliot's "The Love Song of J. Alfred Prufrock": "Shall I say, I have gone at dusk through narrow streets / And watched the smoke that rises from the pipes / Of lonely men in shirt-sleeves, leaning out of windows? . . ."

11. At one point in the film, Crawford alludes to the FBI's traditional bias in this respect when he says to Clarice, "I remember you from my seminar at UVa. You grilled me pretty hard as I recall on the bureau's civil rights record in the Hoover years."

12. Harris, *Silence of the Lambs*, 21.

13. Ibid., 22.

14. In Harris's book, the following exchange, which confirms Lecter's elitist attitude, occurs.

Lecter: May I call you Clarice?

Clarice: Yes. I think I'll just call you—

Lecter: Dr. Lecter—that seems most appropriate to your age and station. (Harris, 60)

15. This darkness is literalized when Clarice enters a dimly lit room during an FBI training session that, ironically, prepares her for a replay of these conditions during her basement pursuit of Gumb, right down to the fact that during the training session Clarice is threatened by someone with a gun, who, like Gumb, is standing closer to the camera than Clarice and points the gun at her head.

16. Demme interview, appendix A.

11. Love and Death

1. See, for example, Richard Corliss in *Time*, Dec. 27, 1993, 71–72; and the review in *Newsweek*, Dec. 27, 1993, 46. A strong, appreciative review is offered by Anthony Lane in *The New Yorker*, Dec. 27, 1993, 148–50.

2. Stuart Klawans, "Holiday Wrap-up," in *The Nation*, Jan. 3/10, 1994, 31–32.

3. Ibid., 31.

4. *Newsweek*, Dec. 27, 1993, 46.

5. Corliss review, 71.

6. Ibid., 72.

7. Ibid. In this respect, Corliss's review is representative.

8. Ibid.

9. William Butler Yeats, "Sailing to Byzantium," 11, 22–23.

10. Springsteen's song, "Streets of Philadelphia," garnered for the film its second Academy Award.

11. It's interesting, though, that Miller only *assumes* that, because Andy has AIDS, he must be gay, another subtle point that the film makes about the illogical nature of prejudice.

12. Viewers should note that when Andy passes the reference book in which this ruling is contained over to Joe, Joe pauses before touching it. The action recalls the point during the scene in Joe's office when Joe, fearful of contracting AIDS by touch, was upset after shaking hands with Andy, who then placed his hat on Joe's desk and picked up one of his cigars. In the law library scene, though, Joe (after a short delay) pulls the book toward him and begins to read from it, a very subtle but quite significant indication that at least some of his feelings about dealing with people with AIDS (which were based on ignorance) have changed.

13. During the scene in which Andy is promoted, Wheeler is also revealed as a blatant materialist, a quality in strong contrast to *Philadelphia*'s accent on impalpable emotions like love and trust. When Andy

thanks Wheeler for his faith in him, Wheeler says that faith has nothing to do with it, defining the term as believing in something for which one has no evidence, and stressing that the firm promoted Andy on the basis of his performance. Nonetheless, Wheeler shares Andy and Joe's belief in the law as an ideal.

14. Although mirrors as a characterizing device also appear in *Swing Shift* and *Married to the Mob* (*Something Wild*'s Ray saw himself in a mirror, but no awareness resulted from this action), in *Philadelphia* their significance is inverted. Where in the earlier films characters looked into mirrors and achieved a degree of self-recognition, in this film mirrors are used as an indication of what other people are going to think of Andy. Thus, when Andy early in the film checks the makeup that he's using to hide his KS lesions, and when, later, he looks at himself in the mirror during the trial, the emphasis is, predominantly, on how the lesions are perceived by others. However, it is significant that in the trial scene, Andy has apparently passed beyond his earlier attitude of dissimulation and attendant self-deception to an acceptance of his disease's disfiguring aspects.

15. The phrase comes from Albert Camus.

16. Klawans, "Holiday Wrap-up," 31.

17. Viewers of the film who look closely will also notice that one of the partners of Wyant and Wheeler, Bob Seidman (who was the most sympathetic to Andy during the trial), is also in attendance at this event.

Appendix A. On Set and Beyond

1. The film was released in 1991 as *Cousin Bobby*.

Filmography

Caged Heat (Renegade Girls) (1974)

DIRECTION: Jonathan Demme
SCRIPT: Jonathan Demme
CINEMATOGRAPHY: Tak Fujimoto
EDITING: Johanna Demetrakas, Carolyn Hicks, Michael Goldman
MUSIC: John Cale
SOUND: Alex Vanderkan
MAKEUP: Rhavon
EXECUTIVE PRODUCER: S. W. Gelfman
PRODUCER: Evelyn Purcell
DISTRIBUTOR: New World Pictures

CAST: Erica Gavin (Wilson), Roberta Collins (Belle), Juanita Brown (Maggie), Ella Reid (Pandora), Rainbeaux Smith (Lavelle), Barbara Steele (Superintendent McQueen), Warren Miller (Dr. Randolph), Don Heitzer (Arresting Narc), Mike Shack (Jake), Gary Goetzman (Sparky), John Aprea (Dream Man), Ginna Martino (Dream Guard), Irene Stokes (Hazel), Cynthia Songey (Hazel), Ann Stockdale (Bonnie), Amy Barrett (Amy), Cydoni Cale (Cindy), Deborah Clearbranch (Debbie), Essie Hayes (Essie), Valley Hoffman (Val), Cicely Johnston (Cicely), Carol Miller (Carol), Vi Oliphant (Vi), Gwen Sawe (Gwen), Susan Nelson, Kathy Jordan (New Prisoners), Toby Carr Rafelson (Pinter), Layla Gallaway (Shower Guard), Jack O'Riley, Hugh Corcoran, Jim Watkins, Bob Fontaine (Sharpshooters), David O. (Captain), Dorothy Love (Kitchen Matron), Carol Terry (Kitchen Guard), Leslie Otis (Station Mechanic), Patrick Wright (Cop at Gas Station), Sharon, George, and Brent Armitage (Family in Car), Keesha (Dog in Car), Lynda Gold (Crazy Alice), Carmen Argenziano (Undercover Wrestler), Rob Reece (Mickey Mouse Robber), Stuart Brandt (Donald Duck Robber), Bruce Pern (Getaway Driver), Gary Littlejohn (Cop at Bank), Hal Marshall (Bank Guard), Marsha K. Viola, Stephanie (Liberated Prisoners), Joe Viola (Sports Car Driver), Mike Gray (Gate Guard)

Crazy Mama (1975)

DIRECTION: Jonathan Demme
SCRIPT: Richard Thom, from a story by Frances Doel
CINEMATOGRAPHY: Bruce Logan
EDITING: Allan Holzman, Lewis Teague
MUSIC: Snotty Scott and the Hankies
SOUND MIXER: Bob Mishakorall
MAKEUP: Charlene Roberson
PRODUCER: Julie Corman
DISTRIBUTOR: New World Pictures

CAST: Cloris Leachman (Melba), Stuart Whitman (Joe Bob), Ann Sothern (Sheba), Jim Backus (Mr. Albertson), Donn Most (Shawn), Linda Purl (Cheryl), Brian Englund (Snake), Merle Earle (Bertha), Sally Kirkland (Ella Mae), Clint Kimbrough (Daniel), Dick Miller (Wilbur Janeway), Carmen Argenziano (Supermarket Manager), Harry Northup (FBI Man), Ralph James (The Sheriff, 1932), Dinah Englund (Melba, 1932), Robert Reece (Mover), Mickey Fox (Mrs. Morgan), John Aprea (Marvin), Cynthia Songey (Lucinda), Hal Marshall (Bartender), Beach Dickerson (Desk Clerk), Barbara Ann Walters (Lady Teller), Bill McLean (Bank Manager), William Luckey (Newsman), Warren Miller (Justice of the Peace), Saul Kingman (Col. Snodgrass), Vince Barnett (Homer), Tisha Sterling (Sheba, 1932)

Fighting Mad (1976)

DIRECTION: Jonathan Demme
SCRIPT: Jonathan Demme
CINEMATOGRAPHY: Michael Watkins
EDITING: Anthony Magro
MUSIC: Bruce Langhorne
PRODUCER: Roger Corman
DISTRIBUTOR: Twentieth-Century Fox

CAST: Peter Fonda (Tom Hunter), Gino Franco (Dylan Hunter), Harry Northup (Sheriff Len Skerritt), Philip Carey (Pierce Crabtree), Noble Willingham (Senator Hingle), John Doucette (Jeff Hunter), Scott Glen (Charlie Hunter), Lynn Lowry (Lorene Maddox), Kathleen Miller (Carolee Hunter), Ted Markland (Hal Fraser), Laura Wetherford, Gerry Wetherford (Fraser children), Peter Fain (Gillette), Allan Wyatt (Judge O'Connor)

Citizens Band (Handle with Care) (1977)

DIRECTION: Jonathan Demme
SCRIPT: Paul Brickman

CINEMATOGRAPHY: Jordan Cronenweth
EDITING: John F. Link II
MUSIC: Bill Conti
SOUND MIXER: Gene Cantamessa
MAKEUP: Gary Morris
PRODUCER: Freddie Fields
DISTRIBUTOR: Paramount Pictures

CAST: Paul Le Mat ("Spider"), Candy Clark ("Electra"), Bruce McGill ("Blood"), Roberts Blossom ("Papa Thermodyne"), Tramp ("Ned the Dog"), Charles Napier (Chrome Angel), Ann Wedgeworth (Dallas Angel), Marcia Rudd (Portland Angel), Alix Elias (Hot Coffee), Richard Bright (Smilin' Jack), Ed Begley, Jr. (The Priest), Michael Rothman (Cochise), Michael Mahler (The Hustler), Harry Northup (The Red Baron), Will Seltzer (Warlock), Leila Smith ("Grandma Breaker"), Micki Mann (Hustler's Mother), Roy Hollis (Shortstack), Gary Goetzman (RV Salesman), Arthur French (Tony), Robert Reece (Les), and the voice of Arthur Godfrey

Last Embrace (1979)

DIRECTION: Jonathan Demme
SCRIPT: David Shuber, based on the novel *The 13th Man* by Murray Teigh Bloom
CINEMATOGRAPHY: Tak Fujimoto
EDITING: Barry Malkin
MUSIC: Miklos Rozsa
SOUND: Les Lazarowitz
MAKEUP: Max Henriquez
PRODUCERS: Michael Taylor, Dan Nigutow
DISTRIBUTOR: United Artists

CAST: Roy Scheider (Harry Hannan), Janet Margolin (Ellie Fabian), John Glover (Richard Peabody), Sam Levene (Sam Urdell), Charles Napier (Dave Quittle), Christopher Walken (Eckart), Jacqueline Brookes (Dr. Coopersmith), David Margulies (Rabbi Drexel), Marcia Rudd (Adrian), Gary Goetzman (Tour Guide), Lou Gilbert (Rabbi Jacobs), Mandy Patinkin (First Commander), Max Wright (Second Commander), Sandy McLeod (Dorothy Hannan), Burt Santon, Joe Spinell, Jim McBride (Men in Cantina), Cynthia Schrader (Adrian's Friend), Saana von Scherfer (Shopgirl), George Hillman (Ukulele Player), Gary Gunter (Newscaster)

Melvin and Howard (1980)

DIRECTION: Jonathan Demme
SCRIPT: Bo Goldman

CINEMATOGRAPHY: Tak Fujimoto
EDITING: Craig McKay
MUSIC: Bruce Langhorne
SOUND: David Ronne
PRODUCTION DESIGN: Toby Rafelson
MAKEUP: Dorothy Pearl
PRODUCERS: Art Linson, Don Phillips
DISTRIBUTOR: Universal Pictures

CAST: Jason Robards (Howard Hughes), Paul Le Mat (Melvin Dummar), Elizabeth Cheshire (Darcy Dummar), Mary Steenburgen (Lynda Dummar), Chip Taylor (Clark Taylor), Melvin E. Dummar (Bus Depot Counterman), Michael J. Pollard (Little Red), Denise Galek (Lucy), Gene Borkan (First Go-Go Dancer), Leslie Margaret Burton, Wendy Lee Couch, Marguerite Baerski, Janice King, Deborah Ann Klein, Theodora Thomas (Go-Go Dancers), Gloria Grahame (Mrs. Sisk), Elise Hudson (Easy Street Singer "Rocky"), Robert Ridgely (Wally "Mr. Love" Williams), Susan Peretz (Chapel Owner), Robert Wentz (Justice of the Peace), Hal Marshall (Hal), Nardee Reynolds (Woman Witness), Herbie Vaye (Man Witness), Charles Napier (Ventura), Jack Kehoe (Jim Delgado), Pamela Reed (Bonnie Dummar), Sonny Davis (Milkman George), Brendan Kelly (Milkman Ralph), Danny Tucker (Milkman Pete), Shirley Washington (Patient Debbie), Cheryl Smith (Patient Ronnie), Jason Ball, Darrell Devlin (The Bait Brothers), Danny Darle (Easy Street Announcer), Linda Cardoso, Melanie Prophet, Garrie Kelly (Easy Street Models), John Thundercloud (Chief Thundercloud), Martine Beswicke (Realty Agent), Charlene Holt (Mrs. Worth), Melissa Williams (Sherry Dummar), Anthony Alda (Terry), James Lyle Strong (Gas Station Customer), Rick Lenz (Melvin's Lawyer), Gary Goetzman (Melvin's Cousin Fred), John M. Levin (Reporter), Kathleen Sullivan (Reporter), Jack Verbois (Holdup Man), Robert Reece (Lynda's Husband), Joseph Reyno (First Attorney—Maxwell), John Glover (Second Attorney—Freese), Dabney Coleman (Judge Keith Hayes), Charles Horden (Bailiff), Joseph Walker, Jr. (Third Attorney)

Who Am I This Time? (1982)

DIRECTION: Jonathan Demme
SCRIPT: Morton Neal Miller, from the Kurt Vonnegut, Jr. story.
CINEMATOGRAPHY: Paul Von Brack
EDITING: Marc Leif
MUSIC: John Cale
PRODUCER: Morton Neal Miller
DISTRIBUTOR: Rubicon Films

CAST: Susan Sarandon (Helene Shaw), Christopher Walken (Harry Nash), Robert Ridgely (George Johnson), Dorothy Patterson (Dorothy), Caitlin Hart (Lydia), Les Podewell (Les), Aaron Freeman (Andrew), Jerry Vile (Albert), Paula Frances (Minnie), Mike Bacarella (Stage Manager), Ron Parady (Vern), Debbi Hopkins (Christie), Maria Todd (Heather), Sandi McLeod (Flirt #1), Edie Vonnegut (Flirt #2)

Swing Shift (1983)

DIRECTION: Jonathan Demme
SCRIPT: Rob Morton
CINEMATOGRAPHY: Tak Fujimoto
EDITING: Craig McKay
MUSIC: Patrick Williams
SOUND: Charles L. Campbell
PRODUCTION DESIGN: Peter Jamison
MAKEUP: Thomas Case, Gerald O'Dell
HAIRSTYLES: Kathryn Bondell, Kim Samson
PRODUCER: Jerry Bick
DISTRIBUTOR: Warner Bros.

CAST: Goldie Hawn (Kay Walsh), Kurt Russell (Lucky Lockhart), Christine Lahti (Hazel Zanussi), Fred Ward (Biscuits Toohey), Ed Harris (Jack Walsh), Sudie Bond (Annie), Holly Hunter (Jeannie Sherman), Patty Maloney (Laverne), Lisa Pelikan (Violet Mulligan), Susan Peretz (Edith Castle), Joey Aresco (Johnny Bonnano), Morris "Tex" Biggs (Clarence), Reid Cruickshanks (Spike), Daniel Dean Darst (Deacon), Dennis Fimple (Rupert George), Christopher Lemmon (Lt. O'Connor), Charles Napier (Morris Willens), Stephen Tobolowsky (French de Mille), Laura Hawn (Ethel), Marvin Miller (Rollo), Susan Barnes (Skinny), Beth Henley (Bible pusher), Gene Borkman (MP at embarkation), Alana Stewart (Frankie Parker), Philip Cristin (Pervert at Egyptian), Penny Johnson (Genevieve), Isabell Monk (Rita), Maggie Renzi (First interviewer), Sandy McLeod (Second interviewer), George Schwartz (Cribman), Alan Toy (Assistant Cribman), Oceana Mara (Ladies' room inspector), Richard K. Way (Factory soldier), Harold Jackson (Piano player at Sorrentino's), Don Carrara (Drunk sailor), Todd Allen (Cpl. Bobby Danzig), Gary Goetzman ("Swing Shift" Bandleader), Belinda Carlisle (Jamboree Singer), Lissette La Corn (Peggy [age 3]), Jessica Gaynes (Peggy [age 7]), Deena Maive (Paper girl), Roger Rock (Bellhop), Joseph Hutton (Seaman Amizia), Harry Northup (New Year's Eve marine #1), David B. Carlton (New Year's Eve marine #2), Lisa Chadwick (Vocalist at Kelly's), Eddie Smith (Waiter at Kelly's), Eugene W. Jackson (Bartender at Kelly's), Chino "Fats" Williams (Bouncer at Kelly's), Belita

Max (Mabel Stoddard), Stephen Tobolowsky (Documentary Narrator), Roger Corman (Mr. MacBride)

Stop Making Sense (1984)

DIRECTION: Jonathan Demme
CINEMATOGRAPHY: Jordan Cronenweth
EDITING: Lisa Day
SOUND: Steve Maslow, Joel Moss, Walter A. Gest
PRODUCTION DESIGN: Sandy McLeod
PRODUCER: Gary Goetzman
DISTRIBUTOR: Island Alive/Cinecom International
WITH: Bernie Worell, Alex Weir, Steve Scales, Lynn Mabry, Edna Holt, Tina Weymouth, Jerry Harrison, Chris Frantz, David Byrne

Something Wild (1986)

DIRECTION: Jonathan Demme
SCRIPT: E. Max Frye
CINEMATOGRAPHY: Tak Fujimoto
EDITING: Craig McKay
MUSIC: John Cale, Laurie Anderson
SOUND: Frank Grazia Dei, Tom Fleischman, Les Lazarowitz
PRODUCTION DESIGN: Norma Moriceau
MAKEUP: Richard Dean
HAIR DESIGN: Alan D'Anderio
PRODUCERS: Jonathan Demme, Kenneth Utt
EXECUTIVE PRODUCER: Edward Saxon
DISTRIBUTOR: Orion Pictures
CAST: Jeff Daniels (Charles Driggs), Melanie Griffith (Audrey Hankel), Ray Liotta (Ray Sinclair), George Schwartz (Counter Man), Leib Lensky (Frenchy), Tracey Walter (The Country Squire), Maggie T. (Country Squire Bulldog), Patricia Falkenmann (Charlie's Secretary), Sandy McLeod (Graves' Secretary), Robert Ridgely (Richard Graves), Buzz Kilman (TV Newscaster), Kenneth Utt ("Dad"), Adelle Lutz ("Rose"), Charles Napier (Irate Chef), Jim Roche (Motel Philosopher), John Sayles (Motorcycle Cop), John Waters (Used Car Guy), The Texas Kid (Hitchhiking Cowboy), Byron D. Hutcherson, Eleana Hutcherson (Hitchhiking Kids), Thomas Cavano (Guitar Player), Dorothy Demme, Emma Byrne (Junk Store Gals), Dana Preu ("Peaches"), Max the Dog (himself), Mary Ardella Drew (Donna Pensky), Joseph Lee Davis (James Williams), Edward Saxon (Kevin Stroup), The Feelies (The Willies), James Hurd, Joanna Kitchen-Hurd (Stylish Reunion Couple), Jack Gilpin (Larry Dillman), Su Tissue (Peggy Dillman), Gary Goetzman (Guido Paonessa), Margaret Colin

(Irene), Chloe Amateau (Chloe), Sung Chau (Robbery Victim), The Crew (Gas Station Rappers), Steve Scales ("Nelson"), John Montgomery (Harmonica Slim), Kristin Olsen (Tracy), Heather Shaw (Choir Girl), Vic Blair (Cowboy Maitre d'), D. Stanton Miranda ("Darlene"), Ding-A-Ling (Motorcycle Dog), Johnny Mairs (Motorcycle Driver), George Henry Wyche, Jr., Marilee K. Smith, Jeffrey R. Roux, Jeff Hein (Police Officers), Gil Lazier (Homicide Detective), Anna Lemme (The Girl in 3F), "Sister Carol" East ("Dottie")

Swimming to Cambodia (1987)

DIRECTION: Jonathan Demme
WRITTEN AND PERFORMED BY: Spalding Gray
CINEMATOGRAPHY: John Bailey
EDITING: Carol Littleton
MUSIC: Laurie Anderson
SOUND: Skip Lievsay, Philip Stockton, Christopher Weir
PRODUCTION DESIGN: Sandy McLeod
EXECUTIVE PRODUCERS: Lewis Allen, Peter Newman
PRODUCER: R. A. Shafransky
DISTRIBUTOR: Cinecom Entertainment Group
CAST FROM *THE KILLING FIELDS*: Sam Waterston, Ira Wheeler

Haiti: Dreams of Democracy (1987)

DIRECTION: Jonathan Demme, Joe Menell
CINEMATOGRAPHY: Jean Fabius, Dyanna Taylor
EDITING: Kathy Schermerhorn
SOUND: Eric Taylor, Jean-Claude Flanquin
PRODUCERS: Jonathan Demme, Jo Menell
DISTRIBUTOR: Clinica Estetico

Married to the Mob (1988)

DIRECTION: Jonathan Demme
SCRIPT: Barry Strugatz, Mark R. Burns
CINEMATOGRAPHY: Tak Fujimoto
EDITING: Craig McKay
MUSIC: David Byrne
SOUND: Christopher Newman
PRODUCTION DESIGN: Kristi Zea
MAKEUP: Bernadette Mazur
COSTUME DESIGN: Colleen Atwood
PRODUCERS: Kenneth Utt, Edward Saxon
DISTRIBUTOR: Orion Pictures

CAST: Michelle Pfeiffer (Angela de Marco), Matthew Modine (Mike Smith),

Dean Stockwell (Tony Russo), Alec Baldwin ("Cucumber" Frank de Marco), Mercedes Ruehl (Connie Russo), Paul Lazar (Tommy), Oliver Platt (Ed Benitez), Capt. Haggerty ("The Fat Man"), Marlene Willoughby ("Mrs. Fat Man"), Frank Acquilino (Conductor), Charles Napier (Angela's Hairdresser), Joan Cusack (Rose), Ellen Foley (Theresa), Olan Jones (Phyllis), Jason Allen (Tony Russo, Jr.), Diane Puccinella, Suzanne Puccinella (Three-card Monte Victims), Anthony J. Nili (Joey de Marco), Tara Duckwaith (Tara), Max the Dog ("Lucky" de Marco), Frank Ferrara (Vinnie "The Slug"), Frank Gio (Nick "The Snake"), Gary Klar (Al "The Worm"), Gary Goetzman (The Guy at the Piano), Carlo Giovanni (Carlo Whispers), Nancy Travis (Karen Lutnick), Warren Miller (Johnny "King's Roost" King), Steve Vignari ("Steverino"), James Reno Pelliccio ("Butch"), Daniel Dassin (Maitre D'), Trey Wilson (Regional Director Franklin), Colin Quinn (Homicide Detective), David Johansen ("The Priest"), Marie Karnikova (Frank's Mom), Dodie Demme (Pig's Knuckles Shopper), Gene Borkan (Goodwill Executive), Wilma Dore (Uptown Saleslady), True Image (A Capella Singers), Joseph L. "Mr. Spoons" Jones (Mr. Spoons), Tracey Walter (Mr. Chicken Lickin'), Lezli Jae (Chicken Lickin' Server), Alisen Gordy (Chicken Lickin' Feminist), "Sister" Carol East (Rita "Hello Gorgeous" Harcourt), Pe de Boi (Samba Band), Buzz Kilman (Ruthless Sniper), Chris Isaak ("The Clown"), Kenneth Utt (Sourpuss FBI Man), Tony Fitzpatrick (Sourpuss Immigration Man), Al Lewis (Uncle Joe Russo), Tim O'Connell (Abused Ticket Agent), Dee Dee Friedman (Bikini-clad FBI Agent), D. Stanton Miranda (The Gal at the Piano), Luis Garcia (Honeymoon Suite Bellboy), Janet Howard (Abused Stewardess), Ralph Corsel (Jimmy "Fisheggs" Roe), Bill Carter ("The Ambassador"), Obba Babatunde (The Face of Justice), George "Red" Schwartz (Shotgun Marshall), Ellie Cornell (The Pushy Reporter), Ray Blount, Jr. (The Humane Reporter), Todd Solonz (The Zany Reporter), Roma Maffia (Angie's First Customer), Joe Spinell (Leonard "Tiptoes" Mazzilli), Patrick Phipps (Goodwill Hunk), Carlos Anthony Ocasio (Joey's New Pal)

The Silence of the Lambs (1991)

DIRECTION: Jonathan Demme
SCRIPT: Ted Tally, from the book by Thomas Harris
CINEMATOGRAPHY: Tak Fujimoto
EDITING: Craig McKay
MUSIC: Howard Shore
SOUND: Christopher Newman, Skip Lievsay, Tom Fleischman, John Fundus
PRODUCTION DESIGN: Kristi Zea
COSTUME DESIGN: Colleen Atwood

SPECIAL MAKEUP EFFECTS: Carl Fullerton, Neal Martz
MAKEUP: Allen Weisinger
PRODUCERS: Edward Saxon, Kenneth Utt, Ron Bozman
DISTRIBUTOR: Orion Pictures

CAST: Jodie Foster (Clarice Starling), Anthony Hopkins (Hannibal Lecter), Scott Glenn (Jack Crawford), Ted Levine (Jame Gumb), Brooke Smith (Catherine Martin), Diane Ladd (Senator Ruth Martin), Anthony Heald (Dr. Frederick Chilton), Lawrence A. Bonney (FBI Instructor), Kasi Lemmons (Ardelia Mapp), Lawrence T. Wrentz (Agent Burroughs), Frankie Faison (Barney), Don Brockett (Friendly Psychopath), Frank Seals Jr. (Brooding Psychopath), Stuart Rudin (Miggs), Masha Skorobogatov (Young Clarice), Jeffrie Lane (Clarice's Father), Leib Lensky (Mr. Lang), Red Schwartz (Mr. Lang's Driver), Jim Roche (TV Evangelist), James B. Howard (Boxing Instructor), Bill Miller (Mr. Brigham), Chuck Aber (Agent Terry), Gene Borkan (Oscar), Pat McNamara (Sheriff Perkins), Tracey Walter (Lamar), Kenneth Utt (Dr. Akin), Dan Butler (Roden), Paul Lazar (Pilcher), "Darla" ("Precious"), Adelle Lutz (TV Anchor Woman), Obba Babatunde (TV Anchor Man), George Michael (TV Sportscaster), Roger Corman (FBI Director Hayden Burke), Ron Vawter (Paul Krendler), Charles Napier (Lt. Boyle), Jim Dratfield (Senator Martin's Aide), Stanton Miranda (First Reporter), Rebecca Saxon (Second Reporter), Danny Darst (Sgt. Tate), Cynthia Ettinger (Officer Jacobs), Brent Hinkley (Officer Murray), Steve Wyatt (Airport Flirt), Alex Coleman (Sgt. Pembry), David Early (Spooked Memphis Cop), Andre Blake (Tall Memphis Cop), Bill Dalzell III (Distraught Memphis Cop), Chris Isaak (SWAT Commander), Daniel von Bargen (SWAT Communicator), Tommy Lafitte (SWAT Shooter), Josh Broder (EMS Attendant), Buzz Kilman (EMS Driver), Harry Northup (Mr. Bimmel), Lauren Roselli (Stacy Hubka), Lamont Arnold (Flower Delivery Man)

Cousin Bobby (1991)

DIRECTION: Jonathan Demme
CINEMATOGRAPHY: Ernest Dickerson, Craig Haagensen, Tony Jannelli, Jacek Luskus, Declan Quinn
EDITING: David Greenwald
MUSIC: Anton Sanko
SOUND: Judy Karp, J. T. Takagi, Pam Yates
PRODUCER: Edward Saxon
DISTRIBUTOR: Cinevista

Philadelphia (1993)

DIRECTION: Jonathan Demme

SCRIPT: Ron Nyswaner

CINEMATOGRAPHY: Tak Fujimoto

EDITING: Craig McKay

MUSIC: Howard Shore

SOUND: Chris Newman, Tom Fleischman, Ron Bochar, Steve Scanlon

PRODUCTION DESIGN: Kristi Zea

MAKEUP: Carl Fullerton

HAIRSTYLES: Alan D'Angerio

COSTUME DESIGN: Colleen Atwood

PRODUCERS: Edward Saxon, Jonathan Demme

DISTRIBUTOR: TriStar Pictures

CAST: Tom Hanks (Andrew Beckett), Denzel Washington (Joe Miller), Roberta Maxwell (Judge Tate), Buzz Kilman ("Crutches"), Karen Finley (Dr. Gillman), Daniel Chapman (Clinic Storyteller), Mark Sorensen, Jr. (Clinic Patient), Jeffrey Williamson (Tyrone), Charles Glenn (Kenneth Killcoyne), Ron Vawter (Bob Seidman), Anna Deavere Smith (Anthea Burton), Stephanie Roth (Rachel Smilow), Lisa Talerico (Shelby), Joanne Woodward (Sarah Beckett), Jason Robards (Charles Wheeler), Robert Ridgely (Walter Kenton), Chandra Wilson (Chandra), Ford Wheeler (Alan), David Drake (Bruno), Peter Jacobs (Peter/Mona Lisa), Antonio Banderas (Miguel Alvarez), Paul Lazar (Dr. Klenstein), Bradley Whitford (Jamey Collins), Lisa Summerour (Lisa Miller), Freddie Foxxx, Paul Moore (Hospital Patients), Warren Miller (Mr. Finley), Lauren Roselli (Iris), Jane Moore (Lydia Glines), Joey Perillo (Filko), Bill Rowe (Dr. Armbruster), Dennis Radesky (Santa Claus), Glen Hartell (Library Guard), Tracey Walter (Librarian), John Ignarri, Richard Ehrlich (Young Men in Library), Julius Erving (Himself), Ann Dowd (Jill Beckett), Katie Lintner (Alexis), Peg French, Ann Howard (The Bronte Sisters), Meghan Tepas (Meghan), John Bedford Lloyd (Matt Beckett), Robert Castle (Bud Beckett), Molly Hickok (Molly Beckett), Dan Olmstead (Randy Beckett), Elizabeth Roby (Elizabeth Beckett), Adam Le Fevre (Jill's Husband), Gary Goetzman (Guido Paonessa), Daniel von Bargen (Jury Foreman), Melissa Fraser Brown, Jordan Cael, Dodie Demme, Patricia Greenwell, Donovan Mannato, Harry Northup, Steven Scales, Billy Ray Tyson, Kenneth Utt, Steve Vignari, Lawrence T. Wrentz (The Jury), Mary Steenburgen (Belinda Conine), Obba Babatunde (Jerome Green), James B. Howard (Dexter Smith), Charles Techman (Ralph Peterson), Charles Napier (Judge Garnett), Roger Corman (Mr. Laird), Jim Roche ("Not Adam and Steve"), Donna Hamilton (Angela Medina), Mayor Edward Rendell (Himself), John T. O'Connell (Macho Barfly), Edward Kirkland (Cousin Eddie), Tony Fitzpatrick (Bartender), Kathryn Witt (Melissa Benedict), Debra H. Ballard

(Court Stenographer), André B. Blake (Young Man in Pharmacy), Ira Flitter (Andrew's Friend), Gene Borkan (Bailiff), Jon Arterton, Michael Callen, Aurelio Font, Jimmy Rutland, Cliff Townsend (The Flirtations), Q Lazzarus (Party Singer), Lucas Platt (Robert), Lewis Walker ("Punchline"), Carmen Mahiques (Miguel's Mom), José Castillo (Miguel's Dad), Leigh Smiley (Younger Sarah Beckett), Philip Joseph "PJ" McGee (Child Andrew)

Bibliography

Books and Articles

Benson, Thomas, and Carolyn Anderson. *Reality Fictions: The Films of Frederick Wiseman*. Carbondale: Southern Illinois University Press, 1989.

Blount, Roy Jr. "Adventures in the Demme Monde." *Esquire*, Sept., 1988, 207–15.

Corman, Roger, and Jim Jerome. *How I Made a Hundred Movies in Hollywood and Never Lost a Dime*. New York: Random House, 1990.

DeCurtis, Anthony. "An Outsider in This Society: An Interview with Don DeLillo," in Lentricchia, Frank, ed. *Introducing Don DeLillo*. Durham: Duke University Press, 1991, 43–66.

DeLillo, Don. *Libra*. New York: Viking Publishers, 1988.

di Franco, J. Philip, ed. *The Movie World of Roger Corman*. New York: Chelsea House, 1979.

Doig, Ivan. *Utopian America: Dreams and Realities*. New Jersey: Hayden Books, 1976.

Fiedler, Leslie. *Love and Death in the American Novel*. New York: Dell Publishers, 1966.

Frye, Northrop. *Anatomy of Criticism*. Princeton: Princeton University Press, 1971.

_____. *A Natural Perspective*. New York: Harcourt, Brace, Jovanovich, 1965.

Gray, Spalding. *Swimming to Cambodia*. New York: Theatre Communications Group, 1985.

Harris, Thomas. *The Silence of the Lambs*. New York: St. Martin's Press, 1988.

Lawrence, D. H. *Studies in Classic American Literature*. New York: Viking Press, 1964.

Robbe-Grillet, Alain. *For a New Novel*. Trans. Richard Howard. New York: Books for Libraries Press, n.d.

Smith, Gavin. "Identity Check." *Film Comment*, Jan.-Feb., 1991, 28–37.

Sragow, Michael. "Jonathan Demme on the Line." *American Film*, Jan.-Feb. 1984, 44–47, 80.

Willeford, Charles. *Sideswipe*. New York: St. Martin's Press, 1987.

Wood, Robin. "An Introduction to the American Horror Film" in *The American Nightmare*. Toronto: Festival of Festivals, 1971, 7–28.

Index

A Ph.D. in English from the University of Minnesota, Michael Bliss teaches English and film at Virginia Polytechnic Institute and State University. His previous books include *Brian De Palma*; *Martin Scorsese and Michael Cimino*; *Justified Lives: Morality and Narrative in the Films of Sam Peckinpah*; and *Doing It Right: The Best Criticism on Sam Peckinpah's "The Wild Bunch."* Bliss's forthcoming books include *The Word Made Flesh: Catholicism and Conflict in the Films of Martin Scorsese* and, from Southern Illinois University Press, a co-authored, illustrated volume on the making of *The Wild Bunch*. He is presently completing *Dreams Within a Dream*, a study of Australian cinema and the work of director Peter Weir.

An M.A. in English from the University of Minnesota, Christina Banks is currently doing research for a critical study of directors Tsui Hark and John Woo.